The Art of
Leather Burning

Step-by-Step Pyrography Techniques

Lora Susan Irish

DOVER PUBLICATIONS, INC.
Mineola, New York

Acknowledgments

I would like to extend my deepest appreciation to the team at Dover Publications, Inc., who contributed to the creation of this book: Vanessa Putt, the book's acquisition editor; Janet Kopito, the book's in-house editor; and Jennifer Becker, the book's designer; as well as Marie Zaczkiewicz, Design Manager, Fred Becker and Segundo Gutierrez, who performed the color correction for the book's images, and Susan Rattiner, Supervising Editor, Jim Miller, Editor, and Kathy Levine, Copy Editor/Proofreader, who carefully checked the pages for accuracy, consistency, and continuity.

Bibliographical Note

The Art of Leather Burning: Step-by-Step Pyrography Techniques is a new work, first published by Dover Publications, Inc., in 2017.

Library of Congress Cataloging-in-Publication Data

Names: Irish, Lora S., author.
Title: The art of leather burning : step-by-step pyrography techniques / Lora Susan Irish.
Description: Mineola, New York : Dover Publications, Inc., [2017]
Identifiers: LCCN 2016046660| ISBN 9780486809427 | ISBN 0486809420
Subjects: LCSH: Leatherwork. | Pyrography.
Classification: LCC TT290 .I75 2017 | DDC 745.53/1—dc23 LC record available at https://lccn.loc.gov/2016046660

Manufactured in the United States by LSC Communications
80942004   2018
www.doverpublications.com

Contents

Measurement Conversion Chart

$\frac{1}{16}$" (2mm)

$\frac{1}{8}$" (3mm)

$\frac{3}{16}$" (5mm)

$\frac{1}{4}$" (6mm)

$\frac{5}{16}$" (8mm)

$\frac{25}{64}$" (10mm)

$\frac{1}{2}$" (13mm)

$\frac{5}{8}$" (16mm)

$\frac{3}{4}$" (19mm)

$\frac{7}{8}$" (21mm)

1" (25mm)

1$\frac{1}{16}$" (27mm)

1$\frac{1}{8}$" (28.5mm)

1$\frac{3}{16}$" (30mm)

1$\frac{1}{4}$" (32mm)

1$\frac{3}{8}$" (35mm)

1$\frac{1}{2}$" (38mm)

1$\frac{39}{64}$" (41mm)

1$\frac{3}{4}$" (44.5mm)

1$\frac{7}{8}$" (48mm)

2" (51mm)

2$\frac{1}{16}$" (52mm)

2$\frac{1}{8}$" (54mm)

2$\frac{3}{16}$" (55.5mm)

2$\frac{1}{4}$" (57mm)

2$\frac{23}{64}$" (60mm)

2$\frac{1}{2}$" (63.5mm)

2$\frac{41}{64}$" (67mm)

2$\frac{3}{4}$" (70mm)

2$\frac{7}{8}$" (73mm)

3" (77mm)

3$\frac{1}{4}$" (83mm)

3$\frac{1}{2}$" (90mm)

3$\frac{3}{4}$" (96mm)

4" (102mm)

4$\frac{1}{4}$" (108mm)

4$\frac{1}{2}$" (115mm)

4$\frac{3}{4}$" (121mm)

5" (127mm)

5$\frac{3}{4}$" (146mm)

6" (152mm)

6$\frac{1}{4}$" (165mm)

6$\frac{3}{4}$" (171mm)

7" (178mm)

7$\frac{1}{4}$" (184mm)

7$\frac{1}{2}$" (191mm)

7$\frac{3}{4}$" (197mm)

8" (203mm)

8$\frac{1}{4}$" (209mm)

8$\frac{1}{2}$" (216mm)

8$\frac{3}{4}$" (222mm)

9" (229mm)

10" (254mm)

10$\frac{1}{4}$" (260mm)

10$\frac{1}{2}$" (267mm)

11" (279mm)

11$\frac{1}{4}$" (285mm)

12" (305mm)

12$\frac{1}{4}$" (311mm)

13" (330mm)

13$\frac{3}{4}$" (349mm)

14" (356mm)

14$\frac{1}{2}$" (369mm)

14$\frac{3}{4}$" (375mm)

15" (381mm)

16" (406mm)

17" (432mm)

18" (457mm)

19" (483mm)

20" (508mm)

21" (533mm)

21$\frac{1}{2}$" (546mm)

22" (559mm)

22$\frac{1}{2}$" (572mm)

23" (584mm)

24" (610mm)

34" (864mm)

36" (915mm)

Basic Leathercrafting Supply List

Adjustable stitching groover—hand tool used to cut a shallow line at a pre-set measurement from the edge of the leather

Artificial sinew, waxed thread, linen thread—stitching threads

Craft knife, rotary cutter, bench knife—tools used to cut out the construction pieces

Edge beveler—tool used to "round-over" the sharp outer corners of the leather

Edge slicker—burnishing tool used with Gum Tragacanth

Gum Tragacanth—medium used to seal, slick, and burnish the edges of the leather

Harness needles, tapestry needles—dull-pointed needles used in leather stitching

Maul, mallet, ball peen hammer—tools used with round drive punches; used to set rivets and snaps

Overstitcher, stitching wheel—toothed wheel with pre-set spacing used to make stitching holes

Poly board or thick cork board—pounding and cutting boards

Rotary hole punch or round drive punch—tools used to cut holes for rivets, screw posts, and snaps

Self-healing cutting mat—used for work table protection and grid-work cutting

Sewing awl—tool used to cut holes for stitching

Skiver—tool used to thin the edge of the leather where two pieces are stitched together

Soft #6–#8 pencil—used for marking and transferring guidelines

Synthetic all-purpose eraser—used to clean the leather of dirt and pencil marks

Transparent ruler, metal ruler—used for measuring stitching and hole placement

Basic Leather Kit

Belt buckles, belt keeper staple

Cotton daubers, cotton swabs

Dee rings, split rings, and trigger snaps

Leather bracelet crimp end caps—jewelry findings

Rivets—double capped, single capped

Rivet setters—rivet setter, rivet anvil, domed rivet setter

Screw-post conchos

Suede lacings ⅛" (3mm) and ³⁄₁₆" (5mm)]

Synthetic eraser (all-purpose)

Basic Pyrography Supply List

Assorted grit foam-core nail files for pen-tip cleaning

Document cleaning pad, synthetic eraser, white artists eraser—used to remove tracing lines

Emery cloth—400- and 1600-grit for pen-tip cleaning

Graphite paper—used for tracing

High-range one-temperature pyrography pen

Leather strop and honing compound for pen-tip cleaning

Low-range one-temperature pyrography pen

Pen tips—medium writing tip, wide-ball tip, micro-ball tip, shader tip, micro-writing tip, large round shading tip

Rheostat-controlled pyrography pen

Scissors, rulers, and low-tack masking tape

Variable-temperature pyrography pen

About the Author

I was so thrilled when Vanessa Putt, the Acquisitions Editor at Dover Publications, Inc., called in the early spring of 2015 to propose that I write a book for Dover. I grew up in a household where the pursuit of arts and crafts flourished, and you never bought what you yourself could create. The dining-room table was always full of someone's current project, from piles of fabric for Mom's quilting to pans of oil and bluing for Dad's antique rifle restoration or jewelry work. Our bookshelves were packed to the brim with Dover books that offered ideas, instructions, and patterns, ready to use for that next craft project. Over the years of loving use, many of those books have become dog-eared, have dirty, hard-used pages, broken spines, or loose pages stuffed in the back. But they are still treasured and now reside on my craft bookshelf, with new titles being added all the time.

Having the opportunity to become a Dover author is an achievement that I never expected as a young woman beginning my career in craft book publishing. The thought that this title, *The Art of Leather Burning*, with my name as the author, will soon join the decades of Dover craft books on my art shelf is beyond imagination.

Lora S. Irish is a nationally and internationally known artist and author who currently has twenty-five woodcarving, pyrography, and craft pattern books in publication, including *Chip Carving 1 and 2, Classic Carving Patterns, Landscapes in Relief, Wildlife Carving in Relief, Great Book of Fairy Patterns, Great Book of Dragon Patterns, Great Book of Floral Patterns, Great Book of Tattoo Patterns, Easy and Elegant Copper Jewelry,* and *Wood Spirits and Green Men.* Twelve of the author's purebred dog-breed oil on canvas paintings have been published as limited-edition fine art prints.

Working from their home studio, Lora and her husband and webmaster, Michael, are the owners of two websites: www.ArtDesignsStudio.com, which features Lora's digital arts and crafts patterns, and www.LSIrish.com, where the artist offers free online tutorials and projects.

The Art of
Leather Burning

Step-by-Step Pyrography Techniques

CHAPTER 1

Pyrography Tools and Supplies

In this chapter we explore the basic pyrography tools and supplies that you will use for your projects. The Owl Barrette (page 19), is worked using a one-temperature pyrography burner and a simple outline and solid-fill technique. The Henna Flower Key Fob adds a softly shaded texture-fill background to the outline technique. Detailed shading, texture fills, and outlining are used to create the Wild Rose and Practice Board Journal on page 46. Each burned line or shaded area of a project's pattern drops into the surface of the leather, creating an instant sculptured effect in the burned image.

Styles of Pyrography Units

There are three basic types of pyrography units—the one-temperature pen, the rheostat-controlled pen, and the variable-temperature unit. The style of pyrography unit that you choose depends on your budget, your skill level, and how often you will be burning. One-temperature and rheostat-controlled–style pens are excellent for new pyrographers, as they allow you to experience the full range of the craft without a heavy financial investment. Variable-temperature units give you total control over the exact temperature you need to create values. They also have a wider selection of pen-tip profiles.

One-Temperature Pens

One-temperature pens are readily available at most large craft or hobby stores and are inexpensive tools with which to begin your craft of pyrography. This style is one piece, with the pen and cord permanently attached. The pen is pre-set to reach a specific temperature, and thus is similar to a basic soldering-iron pen. The tips for this style are interchangeable, with threads on the tip that screw into the top shaft of the pen. There may be an on/off line switch on your particular model of one-temperature tool.

> ᴇᴏ **TIP** ᴏᴡ A one-temperature pen can become hot to the touch in the handle area—it may be uncomfortable to hold for an extended period of work. If the pen is becoming hot, simply unplug it and allow it to cool for about a half hour.

Figure 1.1. The one-temperature pyrography pen is a multi-task tool. It has a high-temperature range of around 950 degrees to allow for the heat needed for soldering. Its high range can cause both scorching and excessively deep burn lines; therefore, it is not suggested for leather work.

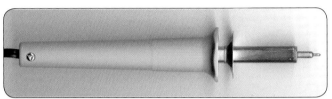

Figure 1.2. The one-temperature tool is specifically made for pyrography work that has a high range of only 750 degrees. This lower heat range is perfect for any leathercrafting project. This is the primary tool that I used for the projects in this book, and it is capable of handling any pyrography technique or skill.

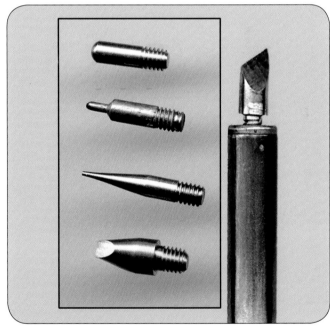

Figure 1.3. One-temperature tools use interchangeable brass tips that screw into the shaft of the pen. Note that the tip of the pen has been left slightly open to show the threading. Five pen styles are available, and these can be used for the projects. The pen is shown with the universal tip, which creates fine lines and wide shading strokes. From top to bottom on the left are the wide ball tip, the medium ball tip, the micro-ball tip, and the square lettering tip.

Figure 1.4. Rheostat-Controlled Pyrography Tool

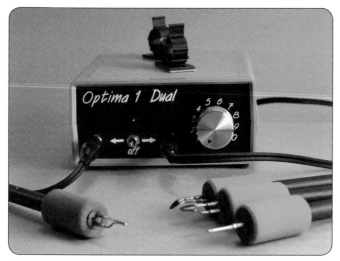

Figure 1.5. This variable-temperature unit is set up to run two burning pens at the same time. The on/off switch allows you to move easily from one pen profile to another with little effort. The temperature range for this unit is far greater than the temperatures needed for burning wood, gourds, paper, and leather. This particular manufacturer also offers several options, including high-voltage cords, and extra-thick wire pen tips for added strength.

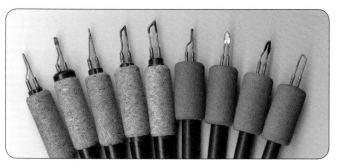

Figure 1.6. These pen-tip profiles show a few of the basic writing, detailing, and shading pens that are available with variable-temperature units. Pyrography pens are made to fit the manufacturer's specific brand of burning unit—therefore, it is not recommended that you use one manufacturer's pen with another manufacturer's burning unit. Check the product information for compatibility on the manufacturer's website before purchasing pens that were not made for your unit.

Rheostat-Controlled Soldering-Style Pens

One-temperature–type pyrography pens are now available with rheostat temperature controls built into the cord. These pens use the same brass interchangeable pen tips and have the same one-piece body styles of the one-temperature pens. The rheostat gives you some control over the heat range, using a dial set for low, medium, high, and hot burns. This type of burning pen gives you both temperature control and interchangeable tips for a modest financial investment.

The simple addition of a rheostat temperature control on the cord of this unit gives you the financial investment advantages of a one-temperature tool with the temperature control of the higher-priced variable-temperature units *(see Fig 1.4).*

Variable-Temperature Pyrography Units

Variable-temperature units give you full control over your pen tip, from extremely cool temperatures for very pale tonal values to very hot black-toned burns. Beyond the temperature range the greatest advantage to a variable unit is that the pen styles allow you to burn comfortably for extremely long periods of time.

Most variable units are multi-task tools that can also be used for acetate template cutting, soldering, and stamping. This style comes with corded pens that plug into the temperature control unit. Pens are available as either fixed-tip or interchangeable-tip pens, with a wide variety of pen-tip profiles.

Which manufacturer's brand of variable-temperature units you choose determines the range of temperature for each unit, the style and grip of the burning pen, and the pen profiles you are most likely to use. Variable-temperature units can be ordered either through mail-order woodworking catalogs or online.

Pen-Tip Cleaning Supplies

As you work your pyrography strokes on any natural surface, the tips will develop a layer of black carbon residue. Carbon build-up lowers the temperature of your pen where it touches the leather, creating uneven tonal values in your lines and texture. If the carbon become excessively thick, it can leave black pencil-like lines on the leather that are difficult to erase.

Extremely fine grit—1500 to 6000—emery cloth, available at most hardware stores, is used for polishing metal. It comes in 9" (229mm) x 12" (305mm) sheets that can be cut into small pieces to fit the pen tip you are using. Rub the pen tip gently across the surface of your emery cloth, returning the tip to a bright, polished look.

Your local drugstore may carry foam-core nail files that have six to seven grit strengths. I keep several in my pyro kit to use when my pens need just a small touch-up for better heat transfer. The heavier grits of these nail files are strong enough to remove the heaviest of carbon build-up without damaging the polished surface of your tips.

As a wood carver I also have a leather or synthetic strop and rouging compound in my pyrography kit. The strop has two sides—one is the raw-leather side up and the other is the finished tanned leather side. Stropping rouge is rubbed over the raw leather; then the pen tip is pulled across the strop to remove the rough carbon particles. To brighten or polish the tip, turn the strop over and work the tip of the tanned leather side.

Figure 1.7. Synthetic and Leather Strops and Honing Compound

> ↪ **TIP** ↩ As shown above, using yellow wood glue, a wooden paint stir stick, and two pieces of 6/7-ounce vegetable-tanned leather, you can quickly make your own leather strop. Cut two leather strips the size of your paint stir stick. Then spread an even layer of wood glue on one side of your stir stick. Lay one leather strip on the stir stick, with the rawhide side up, and press well. Allow to rest for several minutes to set the glue. Turn the stir stick over and adhere the second leather strip to the stir stick with the tanned side up. Place several heavy books on top of your strop to act as pressure clamps, and allow to dry overnight.

Additional Pyrography Supplies

Along with a pyrography pen or variable-temperature pyrography unit, you will need some common craft supplies for the projects in this book. Many of these supplies you will already have in your crafting kit. These include scissors, low-tack painter's or masking tape, graphite tracing paper, and tracing or vellum paper. A surge protector is recommended for use with both the one-temperature–styled burning units and variable-temperature units.

CHAPTER 2

Basic Pyrography Techniques

Basic pyrography strokes include simple outlining, solid-fill areas, and shading using the tonal value sepia colors. Any pattern in this book can be worked in a number of different techniques, giving you a full palette of potential finished projects. In this chapter we will explore which pen tips to use, how each pen tip creates its own unique stroke pattern, and how those strokes can be used to create outlining, shading, and detailing in your burned images.

Pen-Tip Profiles and Burning Strokes

Outlining and Writing Tips

The three burning pen tips shown in Figure 2.1 are used to create even, uniform lines or texture-fills. The loop-writing tip, left, also burns small oval spots for background fill and decorative accents. The ball tip, center, makes even, consistent medium-sized lines and perfect little circle dots in your design. The medium writing tip *(see Fig. 2.2)* creates mid-sized, even lines when held against the leather with a normal, or natural, hand pressure. A light touch to the leather lets this tool tip create a fine detailing line.

Shading Tips

Graduated shading strokes are created using the three pen-tip profiles shown in Figure 2.3. The flattened surface of the tips spreads the heat across a wide area of metal, giving the tip edge a low temperature when it hits the leather. The two pens to the left are used primarily along the curved side edge of the tip. That curve means that your shading stroke has no harsh edge lines along the outer edge of the stroke.

Fine-Line Detailing Tips

Extremely fine lines can be worked using a micro-writing loop pen, the point of your shade pen, or a micro-ball tip cone *(see Fig. 2.5)*. This style of pen tip is perfect for the fine detailing inside the folds of a flower petal, animal fur lines, and cross-hatch shading lines.

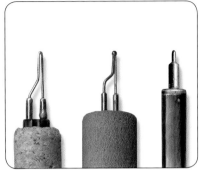

Figure 2.1. Loop-Writing and Medium-Writing Pen Tips

Figure 2.2. Medium Writing-Tip Strokes

Figure 2.3. Shading and Wide-Ball Pen Tips

Figure 2.4. Wide Ball-Tip Strokes

Figure 2.5. Fine-Line and Micro-Ball Pen Tips

Figure 2.6. Micro-Ball Tip Strokes

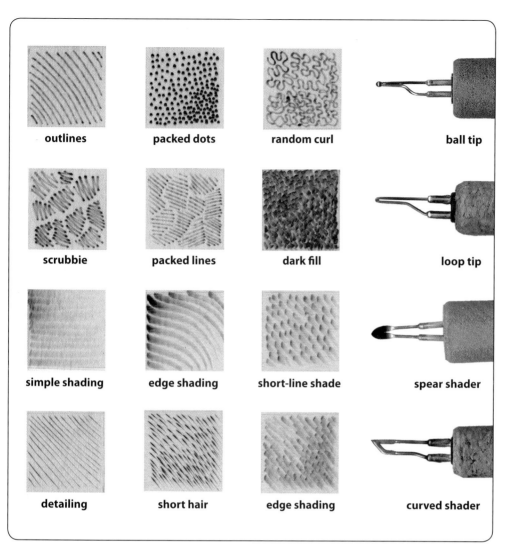

- **outlines**
- **packed dots**
- **random curl**
- **ball tip**

- **scrubbie**
- **packed lines**
- **dark fill**
- **loop tip**

- **simple shading**
- **edge shading**
- **short-line shade**
- **spear shader**

- **detailing**
- **short hair**
- **edge shading**
- **curved shader**

≈ **TIP** ≈ Using a scrap piece of leather, experiment with each of your pen tips to discover the lines, strokes, and texture-fills that you can create. You can make notations on your practice scrap to identify which tip and temperature setting you used to work each sample square for easy reference as you work through these projects.

Figure 2.7. Pen-tip Profile Strokes

Safety

Let's take a moment to consider a few simple safety precautions:

1. Your project media should be an untreated, unpainted, and unfinished natural surface. Paints, polyurethane sealers, varnishes, and chemicals used to treat wood can release toxic fumes during the burning process. Vegetable-tanned leather is suggested for your woodburning leather projects. Leathers that have been dyed or chemically treated should be avoided.

2. Do an Internet search on the media that you will be burning to discover whether it has any toxic properties; there are several excellent data bases available.

3. Work in a well-ventilated area. A small table fan that points toward your work will move the smoke and fumes away from your face. Whenever possible, work near an open window.

4. Avoid laying your project in your lap during the burning steps. This places your face directly above the fumes, increasing your chances of inhaling the smoke.

5. Use a surge protector for your pyrography pen or unit, plugged into a fully dedicated wall socket.

6. Make it a habit to turn off the unit or pen and unplug your burning unit from the wall socket or turn off the surge protector. An unattended hot pen tip can cause fires.

7. While working, set your pens either on the pen stand provided by the manufacturer, on a ceramic tile, or on a large ceramic dinner plate to avoid the pen touching your pattern paper, tracing paper, or any other flammable surface.

8. Pyrography pens can easily reach 750 to 950 degrees and can, if touched, cause severe burns. So if your hands are getting tired or you are distracted from your burning, or if the pen handle becomes too warm to use comfortably, take a break.

Hand Positions:
How to Hold the Pyrography Pen

Hold your burning pen in a relaxed, lightly gripped handwriting position in relation to the leather. Let your hand float just above the surface of the leather with only the side of the hand grazing the work. The more comfortable your grip and hand position, the more even and smooth your burned lines will be.

The pen tip shown in Figure 2.9 has a sharp side edge and crisp ending point that can be used to work extremely fine detail lines. To keep these lines as thin as possible, raise your hand into a more upright position so that as little metal as possible contacts the leather.

Tracing a Pattern

To trace a pattern onto your work surface (in this case, leather), lay a sheet of graphite paper under the paper pattern so that the transfer side is against the leather. As you trace the lines of the pattern, the graphite paper transfers the lines to the leather. Alternatively, you can blacken the back of the paper pattern with a soft pencil, covering the paper completely. Place the pattern onto the leather and trace over the pattern lines, transferring them to the leather. The pencil lines can be removed later on using a white artist's eraser.

Figure 2.8. I use my smallest fingertip as a resting point for the weight of my hand. Having just one anchoring point—that fingertip—lets me pull long, even strokes while controlling both the position of the pen tip and the distance between my hand and the work.

Figure 2.9. Upright Hand Position

Figure 2.10. After the outline of the parrot was burned and the background solid-filled with a dark tonal value, acrylic paint added bright white, greens, blues, and reds to the feathers. Two to three light coats of satin acrylic leather finish were used to seal the leather and protect the paint. This project was worked with 5/6-ounce leather. (See pattern, p. 103.)

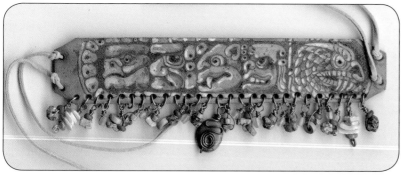

Figure 2.11. You can thin your acrylic paints and craft paints with water to create a semi-transparent wash that adds just a light hint of coloration. The Mayan Wristband was burned using the same technique as the Mayan Boot Belt. White, yellow gold, and raw sienna acrylic paints were thinned by half with water and then washed into the hieroglyphs' faces and stone designs to add just a touch of color without losing the pyrography work. (See pattern, p. 100.)

Figure 2.12. Pink Henna Flower Key Tag

Figure 2.13. Yellow Henna Flower Key Tag

Permanent marking pens add bright color to your leather pyrography. Since they are semi-transparent, medium- and dark-burned tonal values show through the pen ink. Apply two light coats of satin acrylic leather finish to your completed pyrography burn. Allow each coat to dry completely before adding the next. Work your marking pens over the finish to allow the ink to flow smoothly and to create even coverage. Permanent marking-pen colors can be blended by working a paler color over a darker color. The alcohol in the paler color refreshes the darker color, allowing the two to blend. When the inking is complete, allow the project to dry overnight; then apply one more coating of acrylic finish. (See patterns, p. 114.)

Adding Color and Finishes

There are several excellent brands of leather dye on the market that can be used to color the entire leather project or to add color to your leather sculpting or burning. Dyes are alcohol- or oil-based and come as pre-mixed liquids, ready for use. If you choose to use a leather dye for your pyrography work, remember that the dye will change the tonal values as well as the unburned leather used in the project. There are several coloring agents that you may already have on hand—acrylic paints, permanent marking pens, and artist-quality colored pencils.

Before you add either dyes or coloring agents to your finished project, do a test sample on a scrap cut from the same leather as that of your project. Work a small burning on the scrap that contains a sampling of the tonal values that you have used in your larger project. You can now experiment with which type of coloring agent works best for your design.

Acrylic Paints

Acrylic paints can be used to add small touches of bright color to your leather burnings, or thinned with water to create semi-transparent stains for working shading painting. Water-thinned acrylics soak into the vegetable-tanned surface of the leather very quickly, almost instantly, and cannot be blended to create a smooth, even, over-all stain for your leather background. Acrylics used straight from the jar or bottle do not soak into the leather as an alcohol or oil dye and, therefore, can chip, crack, or peel over time.

Pink Petals Key Tag

Intense coloration can be achieved on leather pyrography with colored pencils by using a reworkable spray fixative, available online or through high-end fine-art supply stores. A reworkable fixative has a light tooth or grit texture to its surface after it has dried. You can work three to four layers of colored pencil and seal the leatherwork with one light coat of fixative. The tooth grit now allows you to work three to four new layers of color. You can repeat this process multiple times, creating a fully developed colored-pencil painting with your pyrography work adding the tonal value shading.

Supplies

See Basic Supply Lists, p. v

❖ 1–2½" (63.5mm) by 7" (178mm)-long piece of 6/7-ounce leather

❖ 1 screw-post rivet

❖ Set of 12 artist-quality, wax-based colored pencils

❖ Acrylic spray sealer

❖ Rheostat-controlled pyrography tool

❖ Wide-ball tip, medium writing tip

Figure 2.14. Partial Burning

Figure 2.15. Detailing

Almost all of the patterns available for pyrography today are full, complete designs. Even if your pattern has three full flowers and extra leaves, you do not have to use that entire design. It can be fun to work just a portion of a pattern on your leather project and leave the unworked part to the imagination of the viewer.

1 Cut your key tag out of 6/7-ounce leather. Mark and cut ¹⁄₈" (3mm) holes for the screw post rivet. Use the edge beveler to trim the sharp edges; then use Gum Tragacanth and your edge slicker to burnish the edges. Trace your pattern using graphite paper. (See pattern, p. 113.)

2 Using the wide-ball tip and the same temperature setting you used in step 1, work a layer of pull-strokes in the leaves, moving from the center leaf vein out toward the leaf edge, finishing the stroke about one-half into the leaf. Leave some of the outer edges of the leaves unburned; for the remaining leaves, work a second layer of pull-strokes moving from the outer edge toward the center vein; finish the stroke one-half into the leaf.

3 Set your rheostat or line switch to "off"; allow the tool to cool. Remove the wide-ball tip and replace it with the medium writing tip. Reheat your tool to the original temperature setting. Burn three to five thin accent lines into each petal, working from the flower's center out toward the petal's edge. Burn accent lines along one side of the center leaf veins and side veins. Detail the small flowers that surround the center. Fill the center with loosely packed touch-and-lift dots. Work a second area of touch-and-lift dots in the center to darken one-half of the center *(see Fig. 2.15)*.

4 As shown in Figure 2.15, accent the outer edge of the petals and leaves where they touch another element in the pattern. Those outer edges of the elements that are surrounded by background space will be defined by the background tonal work in the next step.

Use the medium writing tip and the touch-and-lift dot stroke to fill the background space. The darkest point of the background—the area with the densest packing of dots—is at the center point of the overall design. The touch-and-lift dots fade out in the upper left third of the leather (see Fig. 2.16).

Turn the temperature setting of your tool down to a low setting. Using the medium writing tip, work short, loosely packed lines to create a pale tone.

> ∾ **TIP** ∾ Watercolor pencils can also be used on leatherwork. Begin by applying one to two light coats of satin acrylic finish to your project and allowing them to dry thoroughly. Apply watercolor pencils as you would wax-based pencils. Lightly dampen a soft bristle brush with water and work the damp brush over colored areas to blend them. When the coloring is complete, allow your project to dry overnight. Use one or two light coats of acrylic spray sealer over the entire project. Using this spray sealer sets your watercolor pencil work without moving the pencil colors, as a brush-on sealer would. (The step-by-step instructions for the Pink Petals Key Tag are shown on pages 11–13.)

Figure 2.16. Adding color

Figure 2.17. Adding color

Using well-sharpened pencil tips and gentle pressure, work one layer of coloring for each element of the pattern. This first layer will barely show the coloration. Add new layers of color to each element, again using a sharp pencil tip and light pressure. By the fourth layer, the color will have reached a good strength, and you can add small areas of intensity by working a fifth layer (see Fig. 2.18).

- *Petals*—one layer of red, one to two layers of orange, and one layer of white
- *Leaves*—one layer of medium blue near the flower petals, two layers of medium green
- *Center*—one layer of red, two layers of orange
- *Small center flower*—four layers of medium yellow

Dust the leather pyrography coloring gently with a dry, soft bristle brush to remove any particles or loose dust that can develop during the pencil work. Seal the key tag with two light coats of spray acrylic sealer to set the colors and protect the leather.

Figure 2.18. Adding color

CHAPTER 3
Tonal Values

Tonal values, also called sepia tones, are the different shades of brown that you can burn using pyrography. Many patterns use very pale through very dark tonal values to create the highlights, mid-tones, and shadows in the work—this gives an illusion of depth and realism to the image.

Both the Celtic Dragon Necklace and Celtic Knot Necklace depend on tonal value changes in the design to show the overlapping or woven lines that make up a Celtic interlocking line design. By darkening the area where two lines meet, you can suggest that one line tucks under, or flows over, another.

Four tonal values can be seen in the Henna Tattoo Wristband, shown in Figure 3.1. The palest tonal value is the unburned areas inside the center petal rings and the leaves; the second is the pale mid-tone values of the dot-work shading in the outer petal rings. The outlines take on a medium mid-tone of reddish-brown to brown. The darkest value is worked in the background with a solid-fill scrubbie stroke. (See pattern, p. 99.)

The Neo-Tribal Tattoo Wristband *(see Fig. 3.2)* uses mid-toned values in the sides of the cheeks to make them roll away from the high areas of the pale-toned cheeks under the eyes. The nose, left unburned, uses the raw coloring of the leather as the palest value in the burning. The eyes, upper lip, ears, and hair strands use a brown-black tone to push them deeper into the visual space and away from the mid-tones along the sides of the face. Because the tonal value work establishes the sides of the cheeks, the ears, and the hair outlining in these areas is not necessary. (See pattern, p. 103.)

Figure 3.1. Henna Tattoo Wristband

Figure 3.2. Neo-Tribal Tattoo Wristband

NOTE: As you work your Practice Board *(see the Pyrography Practice Board, page 44)*, experiment with these different points. Establish as wide a tonal-value range as possible by varying the temperature setting, the line density of fill-lines, and the pen tip's thickness, stroke speed, and pen pressure to determine which combinations give you the best results.

NOTE: Because there is an unlimited number of tonal values, you may see them described variously as white, pale, palest, pale medium, medium, medium dark, pale dark, medium dark, brown-black, or black.

Figure 3.3. The tonal value scale uses the technique of cross-hatching. Each square is worked with multiple layers of parallel fine lines, and each layer is burned with the lines running is a different direction than the previous layer. The first square is unburned, as the palest value you have is the unworked color of the leather surface.

Range of Tonal Values

There are five simple approaches to creating a wide range of tonal values when working on leather: temperature, line density, pen-tip profile, speed of the stroke, and pressure on the pen tip.

1. A simple line or texture stroke can be changed from a pale tone on a low temperature setting to a dark tonal value by going to a higher setting. Cool temperatures create pale tones; hot temperatures create deep-black tones.
2. Working at the same temperature setting, you can increase the depth of your tonal value by adding more tightly packed lines or by reworking the line pattern over a previously burned pattern at a different angle.
3. Thin-edged pen tips, such as the spear shader, burn thinner lines and therefore paler tones than a loop-writing tool, which burns thicker, wider lines.

4. How quickly you move the hot tip across the wood also determines the darkness of the burned line. Slow, steady movement creates darker lines than quickly pulled strokes.
5. Light pressure on your pen tip burns a darker tonal value than heavy pressure. Because leather is a pliable surface, heavy pressure pushes the tip into the surface, allowing more metal to come into direct contact with the leather. This spreads the heat over a larger burning area, decreasing the overall burning heat and creating a paler tonal value.

Figure 3.4. The design in the pattern above is created by working just the background area, using a graduated tonal value created with a texture-fill that surrounds the dragonfly. Cut one piece of 4/5-ounce leather that measures 8" (203mm) long by 4¼" (108mm) wide. Four distinct tonal values establish the design on this leather belt pocket. The palest is the unburned areas of the flap—the dragonfly and the pattern border. The second value, found in the lower half of the flap, was burned using a random doodle stroke. The third is the darker background area in the upper right side of the pattern, and the fourth darkest value is the brown coloring of the inner pocket leather.

NOTE: The Dragonfly Belt Pocket project was a test sample, a Practice Board piece that I used to establish the temperature settings for my rheostat-controlled pyrography tool. Since I did not start this work as a full, finished project, it has rough-cut edges, quickly worked stitching, and even a few dings from my rotary hole punch.

Dragonfly Belt Pocket

Figure 3.5. Dragonfly Belt Pocket, Front and Back Views

Figure 3.6. Dragonfly Belt Pocket

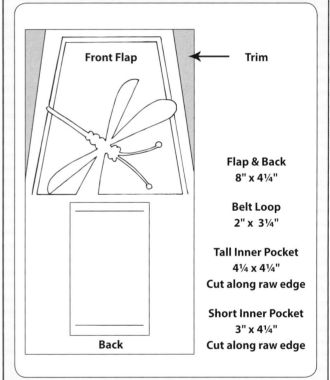

Front Flap

Trim

Flap & Back
8" x 4¼"

Belt Loop
2" x 3¼"

Tall Inner Pocket
4¼ x 4¼"
Cut along raw edge

Short Inner Pocket
3" x 4¼"
Cut along raw edge

Back

Figure 3.7. Dragonfly Belt Pocket Cutting Guide

The simple belt pocket (see Figs. 3.4–3.6) was constructed using scraps from several pieces of tanned leather. The outside of the pocket and the belt loop were worked from 5/6-ounce vegetable-tanned leather. The two inside pockets were cut from 6/7-ounce deep-brown dyed leather. The heavier inside leather, cut along the rough edge of the leather hide, gives the pocket its strength; the light weight of the belt loop leather makes the pocket easy to slip onto the pants belt. (See pattern, p. 103.)

Controlling the Temperature Settings

Figure 3.8. The tonal values in the five leather wristbands shown above are created by controlling the temperature of a one-temperature tool by working the pale strokes as the tool begins to heat; working the medium strokes as the tool nears its pre-set temperature; and burning the darkest strokes when the tool finally reaches its highest setting. (See patterns, p. 97.)

The very pale fill areas in the top wristband are created by plugging in your burner and working with it before it reaches its full temperature capacity. As the burner increases its temperature range, move your burning into one of the darker tonal value areas, or unplug your burner, allow it to cool, and then begin the pale-tone process again.

The Dream and Laugh Bands measure 7¾" (197mm) long x ½" (13mm) wide. The remaining three bands measure 7¾" (197mm) long by ⅝" (16mm) wide. The ends of the leather strips are transformed into bracelets using a crimp-end cap, split rings, and a lobster claw.

TIP Temperature is a primary element for creating pale to dark tonal values. Using the variable-temperature burning unit, you can quickly establish which temperature setting gives you a particular tonal value. One-temperature tools are made to reach one specific heat setting. By beginning your burn strokes before the tool reaches its full temperature, you can work pale tones. As the tool continues to heat, your burn lines will move into the medium tonal value ranges. At full heat you will have your darkest values. To return to the pale values, unplug your one-temperature tool and allow it to cool for about five minutes; then return to your project.

CHAPTER 4

Simple Pattern Techniques

You do not need to be a fine artist possessing well-developed drawing skills to create stunning pyrography projects, especially when working on leather. In this chapter we will look at a few of the basic techniques that you can use to define the pattern lines, create simple shading, and work dramatic black-and-white contrast areas.

Basic Outlining

Figure 4.1. Owl Barrette

The Owl Barrette (Fig. 4.1) is worked from 6/7-ounce leather and measures 5" (127mm) wide x 2" (51mm) high. A large cereal bowl was used as the template to cut the side curves. A ⅛" (3mm) hole punch creates the side holes that support the 6" (152mm)-long bamboo skewer. The pattern was traced to the leather using graphite paper and outlined using a ball tip or medium writing-tip pen. The dark areas in the design were burned using a simple touch-and-lift stroke to pack these areas with small black dots. Finish the project with two light coats of satin acrylic leather finish.

Simple outlining is worked using a ball tip or medium writing-tip pen. Both create an even-sized, uniform line as you pull the tip across the leather. By changing the wire width of the pen tip, you change the thickness of the burned line. Both one-temperature and variable-temperature pens are available in multiple sizes of outlining tips.

The outlining is worked by tracing the pattern to your leather and then burning over each traced line with one pen-tip size. These traced lines can include the outline of each pattern element, the detail lines inside each element, open dot-work areas, and tightly packed areas of background pattern lines. (See pattern, p. 117.)

Figure 4.2. You can use any size writing tip to work a basic outline burning. The wide ball tip creates thick lines that are visually strong enough for very large leather projects. The medium ball tip works well for small projects that use just a few outlines to create the pattern. This pattern, *Made in the USA*, requires multiple lines packed into a tight space in the face and neck feather areas. To keep each line clean, crisp, and well defined, the micro-writing tip was used. (See pattern, p. 114.)

Simple Outlines

Simple outlined patterns can still carry a tonal value effect to the finished leather project. The Butterfly Hat Band uses three strokes—the basic outline stroke, the touch-and-fill dot pattern, and the solid-fill scrubbie stroke. The open dot pattern inside of the butterfly wings takes on a medium tonal value by working the dots in the traced pattern. The leaves and small background flowers also hold a medium tonal value because of the number of outlined, traced pattern lines that are packed into small areas. (See patterns, pp. 104–105.)

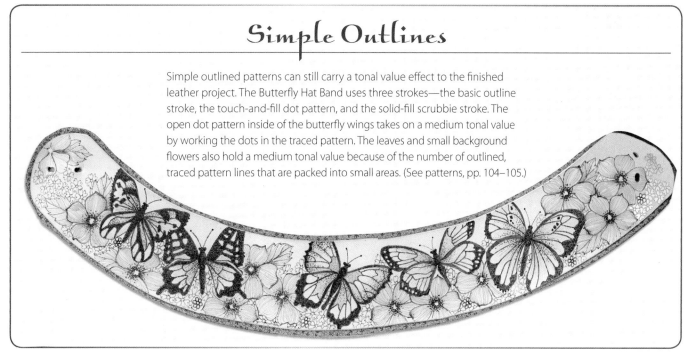

Solid-fill Texture Strokes

Solid-fill areas in your burnings create rich black-brown tones that contrast dramatically with the natural pale tones of the leather. The Celtic knot design in the necklace is created by working the entire background area in a solid-fill dark tonal value. Several layers of burning were needed to create an even, smooth black coloring. In most burning, you will be working the pattern lines and shading inside of each element in the pattern, creating a positive image. Working a solid-fill background and only outlining or shading inside the pattern lines creates a negative image—the image or pattern is set by burning everything that is not part of the image. (See pattern, p. 117.)

Figure 4.3. This Celtic Knot Design necklace was cut from 6/7-ounce leather using a craft knife or bench knife. One-eighth-inch (3mm) holes were punched to receive the 2mm copper chain and $1/16$" (2mm) holes were made for the copper wire bead and chain dangles. Two $1/16$" (2mm) holes were punched along the upper right side edge of the pattern for the copper wire accent link. Use satin or gloss acrylic finish to complete this design.

Simple Shading

Fine lines are burned into each flower petal as the one-temperature tool begins to heat. The shading lines begin at the top of the petal, or where the petal tucks under another petal. Pull the pen tip toward the outer edge of that petal, filling about one-half the area inside of the petal outlines. A second layer of fine-line shading is added to the petals, but worked only in the upper one-quarter of the petal area. To burn the darker lines inside of the petal and to outline the pattern, use the same pen tip and slow your hand motion to give the tip more time on the leather surface. The background, the black daisy center, and the small flower centers are worked using a tight doodle or scrubbie stroke and densely packing the strokes. Rework the background with several layers of burning to create an even solid-fill dark tone.

Complex Shading

In Figure 4.4, the petals first were worked with fine, thin, parallel lines. A second layer of parallel lines was worked on all but the top, pale petals. Small, dark dots were added last in the upper half of each petal, around the lower portion of the flower center and in the leaf where it tucks under the petals. By layering these three texture-fills, pale, medium, and dark tonal values are established, and each area has its own unique textural effect.

> ‹⊶ **TIP** ⊷› Just a touch of simple shading adds depth to the overall effect of your finished design. Fine lines or texture-fill patterns, at a cool to medium heat setting, can be used. Simple shading is often worked without regard to a light source, which would cast specific shadows in the elements of the design.
>
> In the sample shown in Figure 4.4, the shading is worked from the top to the bottom area of the petal, regardless of where that petal is in the pattern. You can add simple shading at any time to your burning. If you have completed the outlining and background fill of the pattern but feel that your design needs more impact, you can lower the temperature setting, or move to a fine-tip pen, to work the pale tones of the shading directly over the work you have already burned.

Figure 4.4. The simple-shaded daisy pattern is worked on a pre-cut 3½" (90mm), 6/7-ounce leather, using a ball tip or medium writing-tip pen. (See patterns, p. 116.)

Figure 4.5. Three different texture-fills were used to establish the shaded areas of the Daisy Key Tag.

Figure 4.6. Extremely fine lines can be worked using the pointed end of your shading tip, a micro-writing tip, or a micro-ball tip. (See Pattern, p. 113.)

Adding Detail Lines

You can work the entire design using fine-line tips, or you can work the basic outlines with a regular medium writing tip or ball-tip pen and then return to each area, adding fine-line detailing using the smaller pointed tips. Small pointed tips also are used to create very small dots and accent spots.

Background Treatments

In Figure 4.9, the Numbered Key Tags, the background was worked using several layers of scrubbie stroke, done with a medium temperature setting and a medium writing tip or ball-tip pen. The first, palest tonal value layer was worked over the entire background space. A second layer was worked in the bottom half, and a third layer was worked in that same area along the outer edge of the pattern.

> ➴ **TIP** ➶ The background area surrounding the pattern is as important as the pattern itself. As shown in the Celtic Dragon Necklace (page 14), the entire image can be worked by burning only the background space and then adding a few detail lines to the main pattern to establish the different elements.

Figure 4.7. Surrounding the number on this 2½" (63mm) x 5" (127mm), 6/7-ounce leather key tag makes the unburned areas in the number stand out from the background more strongly than if the number had just been created from outlines and solid-filled.

Combining Techniques

As you look at the Read With Me Bookmark Owl *(see Fig. 4.8)*, you can see that basic outline strokes have been used to establish the traced pattern lines using a ball-tip pen on a medium-to-hot temperature setting. Next, fine parallel lines were worked at a low temperature; simple shading was added around the eyelids and forehead. The lower area was filled using a doodle or scrubbie stroke, working with the ball-tip pen and a medium heat setting. Still on a medium setting, the background was worked with a solid-fill scrubbie stroke. The final touch, to add impact to the pattern, was to solid-fill the dots, nostrils, and eye pupils with black tonal value worked at a high temperature setting. (Project instructions are shown on pages 94–95. Pattern is shown on page 99.)

Figure 4.8. This project was originally meant to be a wristband, but after the burning was completed, the owl somehow made it into the book I was reading. So now he is my favorite bookmark! This reading-friendly owl was worked on 5/6-ounce leather and measures 2¼" (55mm) wide by 9" (229mm) long.

Working a Series of Projects

Figure 4.9. Numbered Key Tags Series

If you are working a series of leather pyrography projects, do them as a group instead of one at a time. To keep the tonal values the same throughout the series, work each step on each project piece before moving to the next step. That way you will know that you are working at the same temperature setting, with the same hand-motion speed, and using the same pen tip. So, for this series of Numbered Key Tags, I worked the lettering outlining on all four key tags, added the solid-fill to the number on all four, and, finally, worked the scrubbie background stroke on each tag. (See patterns, p. 115.)

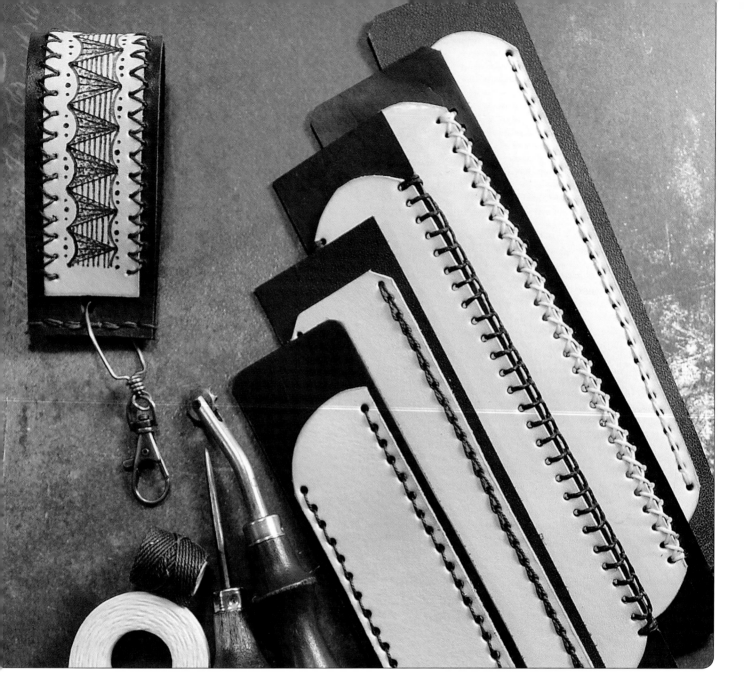

CHAPTER 5

Basics of Leather

The primary focus of this book is on the pyrography techniques that can be burned on leather. So let's take a quick look at the different types of leather you can use, as well as a few simple techniques that will allow you to create artists' journals, boot and wrist belts, and stitched purses. If you are new to leather working, you may want to take a look at the many excellent books available on leathercrafting.

Types of Leather

NOTE: Leather is available in a wide variety of finishes, from unfinished rawhide to brightly colored patterned prints. Goat, elk, deer, buffalo, pig, and even emu leather can be obtained easily from most mail-order leather craft supply stores.

For pyrography projects, you will need leather that has been vegetable-tanned and has no chemical, dye, or coloring agents added. Avoid any leather that has a hard, glossy finish or coloring; vegetable-tanned leather has a soft to medium tone of light beige coloring.

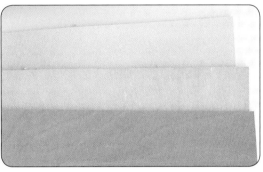

Figure 5.1. Leather is available in many styles, finishes, weights, and textures. Shown in Figure 5.1, from left to right, are 4/5-ounce vegetable-tanned leather; 6/7-ounce vegetable-tanned leather; 8/9-ounce tumbled and waxed dye-finished leather; red synthetic leather; 5/6-ounce pebble-grain dyed leather; a 3/4-ounce suede leather; and a synthetic white 4/5-ounce leather.

Figure 5.2. Vegetable-tanned leather has a soft cream to golden oak color with a matte or semi-matte unsealed finish. The weight and species of the leather can determine the coloring of the finished side. In the figure above, the top leather is 4/5-ounce, the center piece is 5/6-ounce, and the bottom sample is 6/7-ounce. As the weight increases, the coloration from the tanning process deepens.

Mixing Dyed and Vegetable-Tanned Leather

Figure 5.3. Steampunk Belt Pocket (Flap Pocket)

Figure 5.4. Steampunk Belt Pocket (Inside Front Pocket)

Although our pyrography is restricted to vegetable-tanned leather, this does not mean that we cannot work with the wonderful dyed, textured, and patterned leathers that are available to the leather crafter. The Steampunk Belt Pocket is a simple box design with a piece added to the back for the belt loop and a long, overhanging flap in the front, cut from 5/6-ounce dark-brown dyed leather. By cutting the two pockets from 5/6-ounce vegetable-tanned leather, I have two areas for the pyrography, while using the rich color tone of the dyed leather for the main body of the pocket. (See pattern, p. 120.)

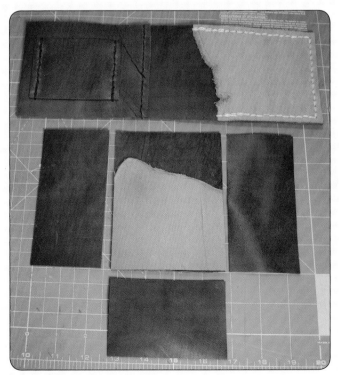

Figure 5.5. Leather pieces cut for the Steampunk Belt Pocket

Leather Weights and Thicknesses

Leather Conversion Chart

Weight /oz.	Thickness/ in.	Thickness/ mm	Common Use
4 oz.	$1/16$"	1.6mm	billfolds, purse linings
5 oz.	$5/64$"	2mm	journal covers, belt pockets
6 oz.	$3/32$"	2.4mm	handbags, cases, totes
7 oz.	$7/64$"	2.8mm	belts, knife sheaths
8 oz.	$1/8$"	3.2mm	holsters, saddlebags
9 oz.	$9/64$"	3.6mm	heavy holsters
10 oz.	$5/32$"	4mm	wide belts, shoulder straps

Working with Leather Hide Cuts

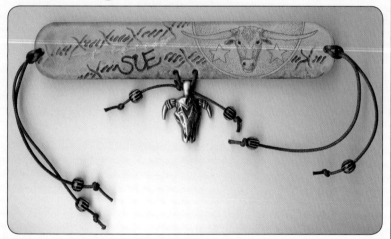

Figure 5.6. Texas Longhorn Wristband

Large hide leather such as half-shoulders and back will have rough edges, branding scars, tanning clamp marks, thin areas, and even cuts and scratches. These are all natural occurrences in any vegetable-tanned leather piece. The Texas Longhorn Wristband, worked from one of those flawed areas of the leather, has a large diagonal scratch left from the tanning process that can be seen in the middle of the left side of the band. On first impression that scratch looked like it could have been made by a barbed wire fence, inspiring an idea for the longhorn branding pattern. (See pattern, p. 100.)

Most large hide cuts have one or two rough edges that are left on the rawhide so that clamps can be applied during the stretching steps of tanning. These areas in the hide are often a thinner weight than the body of the leather. They are wonderful for steampunk and reenactment projects as inside pockets or flap edges. The Dragonfly Belt Pocket, shown on page 16, uses two rough-edge pockets in its design.

How to Purchase Leather

You can purchase small leathercraft kits for pre-cut journals, wristbands, and bookmarks at most large hobby stores. Large kits for purses, leather totes, and saddlebags are available through online and mail-order leather supply companies—these come with everything but the tools needed for the project. These suppliers also carry all of the leathercrafting tools, threads, color dyes, and even project patterns—everything you need to get started.

Surprisingly, leather can be a less expensive media for your pyrography than gourds, basswood plaques, or birch plywood—it ranges from $5 to $15 per square foot based on the tanning process, leather weight, cut from the hide, and hide species.

You can purchase vegetable-tanned leather in large pieces cut from the original hide, which are labeled by the area of the hide from which they are cut—neck, side, belly, shoulder, back, and butt. Each cut is labeled according to how much one square foot of the leather weighs. A 4/5-ounce piece of leather will be thinner and more flexible than an 8/9-ounce piece. One 17- to 18-square-foot shoulder of vegetable-tanned leather side will be sufficient to create all of the projects in this book and will leave you enough leather to create your own designs.

Most of the projects in this book use 5/6- and 6/7-ounce vegetable-tanned cow hide. Vegetable-tanned leather may also come under the names "tooling leather" and "belt leather." The terms saddle, tack, skirting, and sole bends leather refer to heavier weights, 11 to 16 ounces.

While you are browsing about online leathercrafting supply stores, consider one of the many scrap packs that are available. Scrap packs come sorted by the type of leather and the size of the cuts they may contain. A 5-pound scrap bag will give you plenty of dyed, colored, and textured leathers to cut accent areas for belt pockets and small purses.

Leather Patina

Leather, like any other natural surface used for pyrography, develops a darkened patina with age. The leather project you create today will take on a golden-orange or deep beige tone within a decade. Since leather is a long-lasting medium, within several decades your project's leather may deepen into a soft medium-brown coloration—this can affect the impact of your leather burning. The coloration of your pyrography work does not change, but as the leather darkens, the distinction between the burned lines and the leather color narrows.

You cannot prevent the leather from developing a patina with age, but you can delay that effect by using an acrylic leather finish over the project when the burning steps are complete. Acrylic finishes also protect the leather from moisture and dirt. Oil finishes are available for your leather projects, but they can darken the tonal value of the project immediately and permanently.

Water also can permanently change the coloration of vegetable-tanned leather by darkening it one or two tonal values below

Figure 5.7. Here are four examples of the differing coloration of leather hides. The Butterfly Hat Band was worked on 5/6-ounce freshly tanned leather and has a very pale cream coloration. The three pre-cut rounds below the hat band have different colors because of the age of the leather. The dragon round is a freshly tanned piece, the daisy round is from a leather hide about ten years old, and the wood spirit face round is over two decades old. Although the oldest round has dramatically changed color over the years, the burning of the wood spirit face is still quite visible.

the original coloring. If your project requires that some pieces be dampened with water to facilitate bending, do a test sample on a scrap cut from the same piece before starting on your project pieces. If there is a noticeable color change, you may want to dampen all the project pieces at the same time, whether or not you will be bending that piece. This will change all of the leather pieces to the same darker tone.

CHAPTER 6

Simple Leathercrafting Techniques

Let's look at a few of the basic cutting, stitching, and construction techniques we will be using throughout the projects in this book by working a simple boot belt. A boot belt is nothing more than a short version of a standard pants belt. Working through this section will also allow you to create small buckled wrist bands, purse straps and latches, and buckled hat bands.

Figure 6.1. Shown left to right—transparent quilting ruler, skiver, bench knife, edge beveler, Gum Tragacanth, cotton swab, edge slicker, 6/7 ounce leather, all shown on a self-healing cutting mat

Supplies

See Basic Supply Lists, p. v

◈ 6/7 ounce vegetable-tanned leather

◈ 1 belt buckle

◈ 1 belt keeper or one ¼" (6mm) length of leather and belt keeper staple

◈ Craft knife, rotary cutter, or bench knife

◈ Transparent ruler, metal ruler

◈ Soft #6 or #8 pencil

◈ Synthetic all-purpose eraser, document cleaning pad, or white artist's eraser

◈ Rotary hole punch or drive punch

◈ Skiver

◈ Edge beveler

◈ Gum Tragacanth

◈ Edge slicker

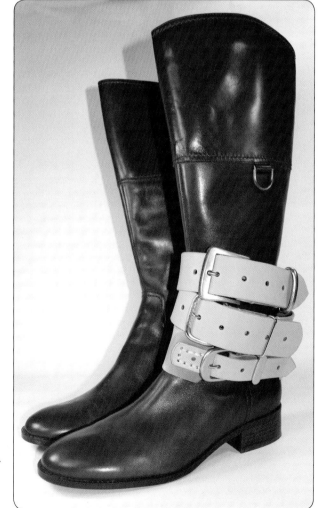

Figure 6.2. Boot belts are as much fun to wear as they are to make. They are just short versions of the standard belt, made to loosely fit around the ankle area of your work or dress boots. Multiple boot belts can be stacked to add to their decorative impact.

Boot Belt Construction

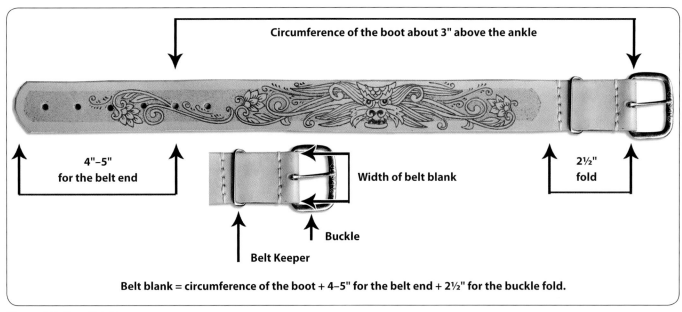

Circumference of the boot about 3" above the ankle

4"–5" for the belt end

Width of belt blank

2½" fold

Buckle

Belt Keeper

Belt blank = circumference of the boot + 4–5" for the belt end + 2½" for the buckle fold.

Figure 6.3 Boot Belt Measurements

Figure 6.4. For wristbands, reduce the belt end measurement to 2–3" (51–77mm); for standard belts increase this measurement to 6–7" (152–178mm).

Measure the circumference of your boot about 3" above the ankle area. Add to this measurement 2½" (63.5mm) for the foldover that secures the buckle and 4–5" (102–127mm) for the end overlap with the buckle holes. This is the total length of your leather piece. Next, measure the width of the buckle where the leather will slide through the bar and latch—this becomes the width of your belt blank (see Fig. 6.3).

Figure 6.5. Purse straps and purse buckles are a version of the basic pants belt pattern. The buckle section, shown bottom right, is stitched to the inside front of the purse, and the hole side is stitched to the purse flap with the holes' tongue extending below the flap to be belted into the buckle.

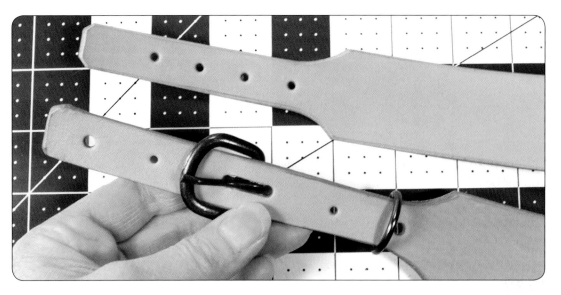

Leather can be cut using a sturdy craft knife, woodcarving bench knife, or sewing rotary cutter. A non-skid, self-healing cutting mat, used to protect your crafting table, comes pre-printed with a measured grid-work and common cutting angles. The metal ruler, shown in Figure 6.6, has a cork back that keeps it secure to the leather. You can also use a T-square or right-angle square. Transparent quilting rulers also have a pre-printed grid that allows you to see exactly where the straight edge of your ruler falls on the leather.

Figure 6.6. Working on a self-healing mat with a pre-printed grid-work will ensure an accurate, straight cut.

A skiver can be used along both out-side edges of the buckle-fold areas on the back of your belt blank from the buckle area towards the front end of the blank. Skivers are used to thin the sides of purse and wallet inserts, purse or belt pocket sides, and any other area of construction that has multiple layers of leather stitched together (see Fig. 6.7).

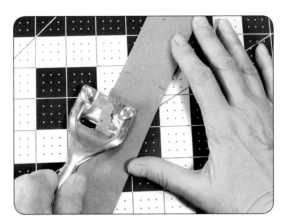

Figure 6.7. A skiver holds a razor-blade edge in a concave curve that removes thin slices of leather from the back edge of the piece. This thins the leather for cleaner edges and easier bending.

When the skiving is complete you can fold the belt blank along the buckle area to check the buckle placement and the thickness of the folded area that will secure the buckle in place (see Fig. 6.8).

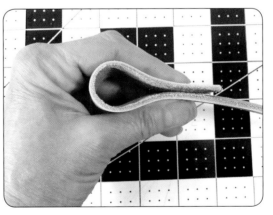

Figure 6.8. In this photo you can see the original thickness of the belt blank and the new edge thickness of the buckle fold. The fold is now about two-thirds of the thickness of the original leather.

The center point of the buckle hole is marked 2¾" (70mm) from the belt blank edge. To create a long slot in the leather through which you will thread the buckle latch, make a mark ³/₈" (10mm) on each side of the center buckle mark. The slot for this belt buckle measures ¾" (19mm) long, total. Adjust the size of your slot to fit the buckle you will be using. Wide, thick metal buckles may need a slot as long as 1⅛" (28.5mm), while small shoe buckles may only need a ½" (13mm) slot. Allow enough length in the slot so that the buckle latch can move freely (see Fig. 6.9).

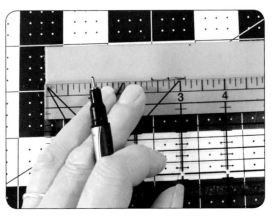

Figure 6.9. Measuring the Buckle Hole

Figure 6.10. Cutting guides can be made out of card stock-weight paper and re-used for accurate, easily repeated hole placement.

Figure 6.11. Punching the Buckle Hole

Figure 6.12. A rotary hole punch has multiple standard-sized hole punches set on a wheel for quick access and hole size changes. The handles are set with an inner spring that helps to drive the punch through the leather surface. As with many quality tools, a rotary hole punch will last for decades—the one shown is from my father's leathercrafting kit and is about fifty years old.

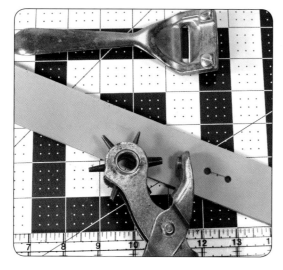

Figure 6.13. Both rotary hole punches and drive punches can damage the underside of the leather around the cut hole. You can avoid this problem by placing a piece of scrap leather under your project leather.

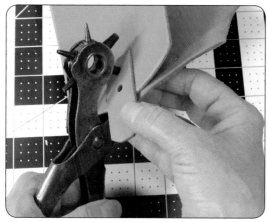

Accessory hardware is often sold in multiple-unit packs. The buckle used in this boot belt came in a package of ten. Since I know that I will be using this style and size buckle in several projects, I made a quick cutting and hole placement template out of a card stock file folder. Note that I have labeled the template so that I know which buckle it matches (see Fig. 6.10).

The two sides of the buckle-hole measured line are cut first, using a hole punch. The size of the punch is determined by the thickness of the buckle latch. For this sample (see Fig. 6.11), the buckle latch measured ⅛" (3mm) wide, so I chose a ³⁄₁₆" (5mm)-wide hole punch, which gives just a little extra room for the free movement of the latch. One hole is punched at the beginning of your measured line, and one at the end.

NOTE: There are several methods of cutting or punching holes. You can use the rotary hole punch, which has multiple-sized punches from a small diameter of ¹⁄₁₆" (2mm), up to a large-sized ¼" (6mm) punch. You can also use round drive punches, which are purchased by the set of four to six standard hole sizes. The drive punch is hand-held in an upright position to the leather, which has been placed on a thick cork board or a thick self-healing poly board, and driven into the leather using a leather or synthetic mallet. Cork and self-healing poly boards allow the cutting edge of the round drive punch or the hand awl to penetrate their surfaces, therefore protecting the cutting edge of your tools.

8. Using a craft knife, bench knife, or straight chisel, cut the top and bottom of the buckle latch slot (see Figs. 6.14 and 6.15).

9. Using a small, round jar or cup as a guide, pencil in a curved cutting line on the end of your belt. Cut along the trim line with a bench knife or craft knife (see Fig. 6.16).

10. Glide an edge beveler along the corner edges of the top tanned side of the leather belt to remove a thin sliver of leather (see Fig. 6.17). This rounds the edge of the leather.

11. Apply Gum Tragacanth along the edge of the belt leather using a cotton swab (see Fig. 6.18). Briskly rub the dampened side with an edge slicker to burnish the leather (see Fig. 6.19). Gum Tragacanth polishes the edge and slicks the fine leather fibers to the side.

12. Slide the buckle latch through the buckle slot in the leather. The latch bar of the buckle rests on the back side of the belt blank (see Fig. 6.20).

13. Heavy-weight leathers may need to be lightly dampened with water in order to easily fold the leather at the buckle latch bar. Avoid soaking the leather in water—this can cause the leather to stain and develop a watermark line where it was drenched. Dampen your sponge with water, wringing out as much water as possible, and then lightly pat the sponge across the rawhide side of the leather (see Fig. 6.21). Gently fold the leather to the back of the belt blank to set the center fold-line at the buckle slot.

Figure 6.14. Opening the Buckle Slot

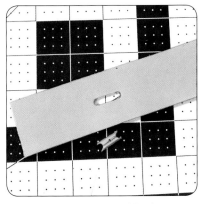

Figure 6.15 Finished Buckle Slot

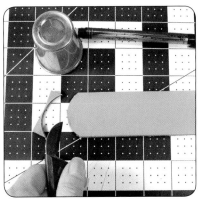

Figure 6.16. Trimming the Belt End

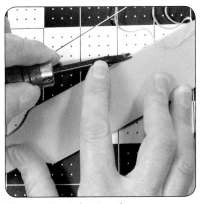

Figure 6.17. Edge Beveler

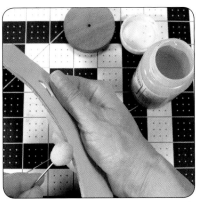

Figure 6.18. Applying Gum Tragacanth

Figure 6.19. Burnishing the Edge

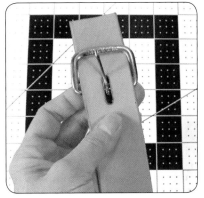

Figure 6.20. Checking the Fit of the Buckle

Figure 6.21. Dampening the Leather

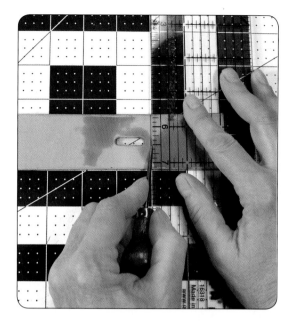

Figure 6.22. Creating a Score Line with an Awl

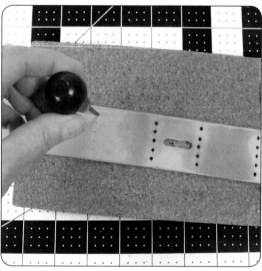

Figure 6.23. Creating the Stitching Holes

 Open the folded end of the belt and align a transparent quilting ruler on its front side *(see Fig. 6.22)*. Create one indent line about ⅜" (10mm) from each side of the buckle slot. Create a second indent line on both sides of the buckle slot 1½" (38mm) to 1¾" (44.5mm) from the slot edge.

With the ruler still in place along the indented guidelines, hold your awl upright to the leather and lightly push the awl to create shallow stitch-guide marks at ³⁄₁₆" (5mm) to ¼" (6mm) intervals along the line. Use the interval measurement that best fits the width of your belt and the leather weight of the blank. Light-weight leathers, 4 to 6 ounces, take a stitching interval of ³⁄₁₆" (5mm). Heavier-weight leather, 6 ounces and up, takes a stitching interval of ¼" (6mm).

 As shown in Figure 6.23, lay your belt on a thick cork board or poly board. Hold the awl upright to the leather with the point set into the guide holes. Push the awl into the leather to create your stitching holes.

Working with Rivets

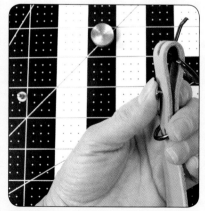

Figure 6.24. Working with Rivets

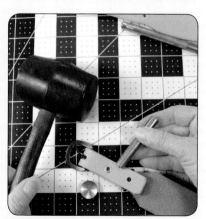

Figure 6.25. Rivet Setter

Rivets can be used to secure your buckle into a folded leather belt blank. Measure and mark the center point across the width of your belt blank on both sides of the buckle slot 1½" (38mm) to 1¾" (44.5mm) from the slot edge. Cut a hole at each center guide mark using a rotary punch set to the punch that fits the width of your rivet post.

Single-capped and double-capped rivets come in two parts. The female part sets into the hole on the tanned side of the leather. The male part inserts into the hole on the rawhide side of the leather, and then sets into the hole in the female part. Rest the female part in the rivet anvil. The rawhide side and male rivet part will face up. Place the rivet setter into the opening of the male rivet part and, with the flat side of a ball peen hammer, set the rivet.

Cut a 20" (508mm) length of waxed linen stitching thread. Thread a harness needle on each end of the thread. Double-needle stitch the stitching line at the base of the buckle *(see Fig. 6.26)*.

 End your stitching on the back side of the belt by sliding the needle through the back layer of leather. Cut the thread, allowing about ½" (13mm) of extra cord. Tuck the extra cord under the back flap. Repeat for the second double-stitching thread, as shown in Figure 6.27.

 Slide the belt keeper onto the belt and center it between the two buckle-stitching awl lines. You can purchase metal belt keepers that match your buckle, or you can cut and stitch your own using the same leather as your belt. As shown in Figure 6.28, use waxed linen thread to double-stitch along the second stitching line. You can create your own belt keeper with a ¼" (6mm) to ³⁄₁₆" (5mm) wide strip of your belt leather by the width measurement of your belt plus ³⁄₈" (10mm) and use a belt-keeper staple to join the cut ends *(see Fig. 6.29)*.

 With a transparent ruler, mark the buckle latch holes on the belt end *(see Fig. 6.30)*. Space the holes between ½" (17mm) apart for wristbands and 1" (25mm) apart for boot and pants belts.

 Set your rotary punch to the size that matches the buckle latch. Punch the latch holes *(see Fig. 6.31)*.

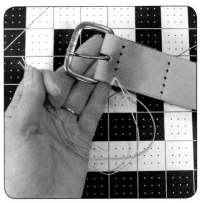 Your completed boot belt *(see Fig. 6.32)* or wristband now is ready to be moved to your pyrography table.

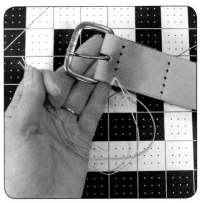

Figure 6.26. Double Stitching

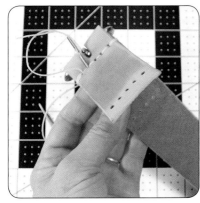

Figure 6.27. Double-Stitch Threading

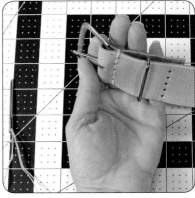

Figure 6.28. Adding the Belt Keeper

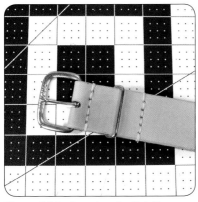

Figure 6.29. Securing the Belt Keeper

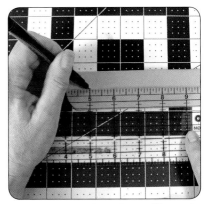

Figure 6.30. Marking the Buckle Latch Holes

Figure 6.31. Rotary Punching the Belt End Holes

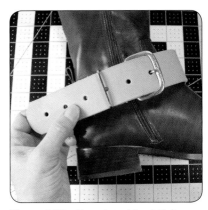

Figure 6.32. Completed Book Belt

Figure 6.33. Double-Needle Stitching—Creating Holes with Awl

NOTE: Because the point of the awl is tapered, the bottom part of the hole will be smaller than the top part. Therefore, press the awl into the leather slightly deeper than you think you may need to to ensure that the needle will easily slide through the entire hole. The pressure used to make an awl hole pushes a small amount of leather into the hole on the top surface, creating a nice, smooth hole. That same downward pressure pushes a small amount of the surface leather away from the bottom edge of the hole. This area can be slightly rough, or ridged. Before you begin your awl work, plan which side of the leather needs the smooth, pushed-in edge, and place that surface upright on the cork board.

> ✎ **TIP** ✐ If one side of your project is made up of two or more pieces, stack and awl-punch these pieces at the same time. The Dragonfly Belt Pocket, page 16, has a front purse piece, cut from the brown leather, and an overlay pocket, shown in vegetable-tanned leather. By stacking these two pieces and measuring and punching them as if they were just one piece, the awl holes are perfectly aligned.

Double-Needle Stitching

The double-needle stitch is the most commonly used method of stitching leather, using a single extra-long waxed thread with one harness needle threaded on each end of the thread. As you work through this project you will see that the great advantage of this stitching method is that when you complete one stitch, the space between the stitching holes on both sides of the leather will be covered by thread.

Harness needles are large-gauged, wide-eyed, blunt-pointed needles that are used to move *through* the leather, not pierce it. In needle crafts, these same needles are called tapestry or needlepoint needles. The thread used in leather stitching comes in several varieties—nylon and polyester waxed, linen waxed, artificial sinew, and sewing awl thread. Sewing awl thread is of a smaller gauge than the waxed thread and is used with a stitching awl. Waxed threads are sold in 4- to 8-ounce spools, or in 25- to 50-yard spools. On average, a simple-construction large purse project may take up to ten yards of thread.

1 Measure a ⅛" (3mm) to ¼" (6mm)-margin guideline from the edge of your leather piece. Measure and mark each stitch using a ³⁄₁₆" (5mm) to ¼" (6mm) spacing. Light-weight leathers use stitching that falls closer to the leather edge and has tighter spacing then heavier leathers. Place your leather on a thick cork board or a self-healing poly board. Hold a small hand awl at a 90-degree angle to the leather, with the point at the stitch mark. Push the awl into the leather to create a small hole (see Fig. 6.33).

2 Cut a length of waxed linen thread 2½ to 3 times the length of the area that you will be stitching *(see Figs. 6.34 and 6.35)*.

NOTE: Working with longer lengths does take some time as you pull the extra thread through each hole; however, it avoids the need to end one thread length and introduce a new piece of thread partway through the stitching.

3 Thread one harness needle onto each end of the thread. Thread one needle through both layers of leather *(see Fig. 6.36)*. Pull the needle and thread through the hole and center the thread so that there are equal amounts of thread on both sides of the hole. As in Figure 6.37, begin the stitching of the pocket in the fourth hole from the top of the pocket. The first three stitches along this side will be worked toward the top of the pocket edge. Make two layers of stitching in the top holes—the top stitch—for a little extra strength. Then begin working down the side, overlapping those first three stitches.

4 Insert the front needle into the next hole in the stitching line; then pull the needle and thread to the back of the leather *(see Figs. 6.38 and 6.39)*.

5 Pick up the back needle and insert it into the same hole as in step 4—one hole above your beginning stitching hole—in which you just worked the first needle. Pull the needle and thread through the hole *(see Figs. 6.40 and 6.41)*.

Figure 6.34. Double-Needle Stitching Needles and Thread

Figure 6.35. Double-Needle Stitching

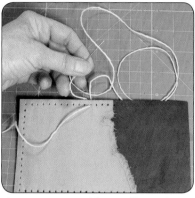

Figure 6.36. Double-Needle Stitching Beginning a Stitch

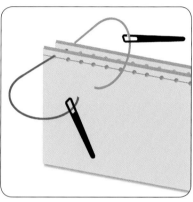

Figure 6.37. Double-Needle Stitching

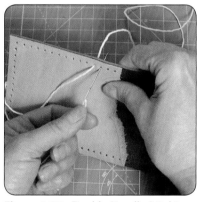

Figure 6.38. Double-Needle Stitching Completing a Stitch

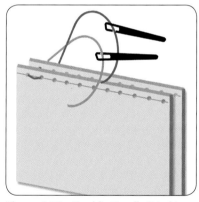

Figure 6.39. Double-Needle Stitching

Figure 6.40. Double-Needle Stitching Working the Stitches

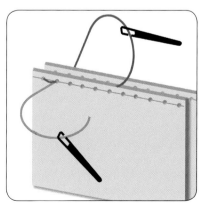

Figure 6.41. Double-Needle Stitching

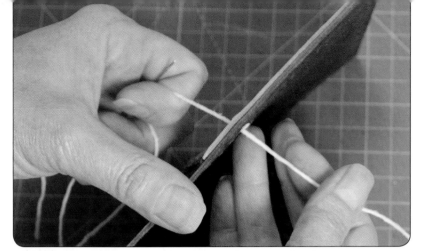

Figure 6.42. Double-Needle Stitching—Stitching on Both Sides

Figure 6.43. Double-Needle Stitching Keeping Stitches Even

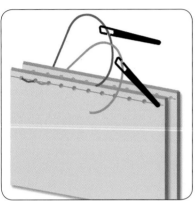

Figure 6.44. Double-Needle Stitching

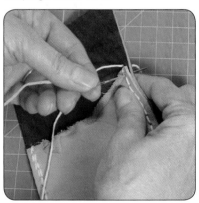

Figure 6.45. Double-Needle Stitching Overlapping Edges

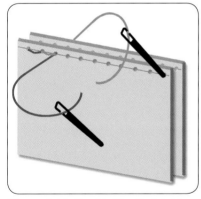

Figure 6.46. Double-Needle Stitching

Figure 6.47. Double-Needle Stitching Ending the Stitching

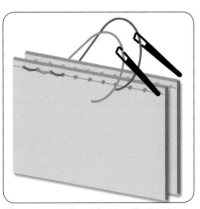

Figure 6.48. Double-Needle Stitching

6 Gently set both stitches into place by lightly pulling off the stitching threads. By passing one needle from the front to the back, and passing the second needle from the back to the front through the same hole, you will create a stitch on both sides of the leather between the two stitching holes (see Fig. 6.42).

7 Pick up the needle that is now on the front of the leather and make a stitch in the next hole. Pick up the needle that is on the back and make a stitch in the same hole (see Figs. 6.43 and 6.44). Each new stitch in the double-needle stitching pattern begins on the same side of the leather in order to keep the stitching smooth and even.

8 Overlapped edges, shown in this top pocket area, and sharp corners can have several layers of stitching to reinforce the area. Stitch up to and through the top stitching hole. Next, work the stitch below the stitching hole; then rework the top stitch. Continue in your original stitching direction (see Figs. 6.45 and 6.46).

9 To end the stitching, work back along your stitching line for several stitches, creating three to four stitches that have two threads per stitch. Place the front needle in the next hole and bring the needle out between the two layers of leather (see Figs. 6.47 and 6.48).

10 Make a stitch, using the back needle in the same hole; bring this needle out between the two layers of leather. *(See Figs. 6.49 and 6.50).*

11 Pull lightly on the threads to set the stitch; then cut the excess thread tails from the stitching thread using a craft knife. *(See Fig. 6.51).*

12 With the back of your craft knife, tuck the tail threads in the space between the two leather pieces. *(See Fig. 6.52).*

Adding New Lengths of Thread to Your Stitching

To add a new thread, work your needled thread until you have about 4–5" (102–127mm) of thread left, total. You will join two new threads around the same area of stitching on your project. Plan in advance to add the new threads in separate holes, spaced several inches apart.

Make one double-needle stitch, bringing the old needle out between the two layers of leather. Slip the needle off that end of the stitching thread. Cut and thread a new length of waxed linen thread with just one needle. Count backwards four stitches along the previously made stitches. Insert the new needle between the two layers of leather and bring it out of the leather on the same side that the original needle was worked in that fourth hole. Work the new needle in the double-needle pattern. Continue working until you are past the last hole for the old needle. With a craft knife, cut both the excess tail of the new thread and the tail of the old thread close to the leather. Tuck the remaining tails into the space between the two leather pieces.

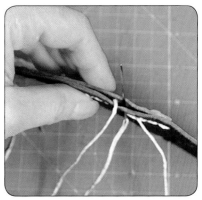

Figure 6.49. Double-Needle Stitching Finishing Stitches

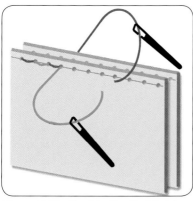

Figure 6.50. Double-Needle Stitching

Figure 6.51. Double-Needle Stitching Cutting Thread Tails

Figure 6.52. Double-Needle Stitching

Figure 6.53. Double-Needle Stitching

⤜ **TIP** ⤝ Because the stitching process entails a great deal of handling of unfinished leather, this area can pick up dirt and excess wax from the waxed threads. Use a synthetic all-purpose eraser to remove the dirt. Remove any eraser dust with a dry, lint-free cloth *(see Figure 6.53).*

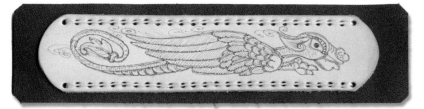

Figure 6.54. The back stitch, often worked in hand sewing, uses one needle on the thread and is worked over two holes per stitch.

Figure 6.55. The blanket stitch, commonly used in crazy quilts, adds a lacy edge of loops to the outside of this wristband.

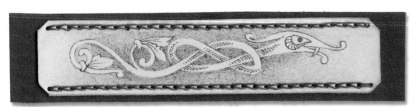

Figure 6.56. The embroidery stitch known as the daisy chain creates a series of locked loops along the finished side of this wristband.

Figure 6.57. This classic cross-stitch pattern is worked in two rows of stitching. The stitches first are worked along the diagonal across the row; then the stitch pattern is turned so that the diagonals are worked back down the row. When finished, the two layers of stitching rise well above the surface of the finished leather.

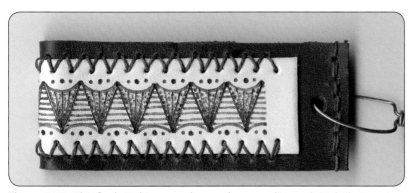

Figure 6.58. This final stitching sample uses the same diagonal stitch that creates the cross stitch, but this time it is worked in the zig-zag pattern.

Leather Stitch Patterns

Just about any embroidery or sewing stitch pattern can be used to accent pyrography leather projects. Have fun looking through your stash of sewing, cross-stitch, embroidery, and even tapestry books for stitch patterns that you can incorporate into your designs. At the left is a small sampling. (See patterns, p. 98.)

Mayan Boot Belt

1 The Mayan Boot Belt uses double-needle stitching with a 1½" (38mm) long by 1³⁹⁄₆₄" (41mm) wide buckle and a 1⅛" (28.5mm) wide latch bar. The belt keeper is made with a 1¾" (44.5mm) steel dee ring. Cut one piece of 6/7-ounce leather 1⅛" (28.5mm) wide by 19¹⁄₆₄" (483mm) long, allowing a 2½" (63.5mm) fold for the buckle area. Follow the directions for making a basic boot belt (see pages 30–35).

2 Using graphite paper, trace the Mayan Boot Belt pattern to your constructed belt, with the repeated flower squares spaced ⅛" (3mm) from the hole end of the belt.

3 The Mayan Boot Belt project uses a low-range, one-temperature pyrography tool and a medium writing tip. Plug the pyrography burner into the surge protector and turn on the switch. As the burner begins to heat, but before it reaches its full temperature setting, start working a tightly packed scrubbie stroke into the background area of each pattern square. Because the temperature is low, this burning will have a very pale, lightly spotted look to the strokes. You may need to turn off your burner, allow it to cool, and then begin the scrubbie stroke again to keep the temperature cool enough to complete all of the squares *(see Fig. 6.59)*.

4 When the pyrography tool has reached its full pre-set temperature, outline the pattern lines for each of the hieroglyphs in the pattern. The pre-set temperature will burn even tones, and an even width line, throughout the entire belt design *(see Fig. 6.60)*.

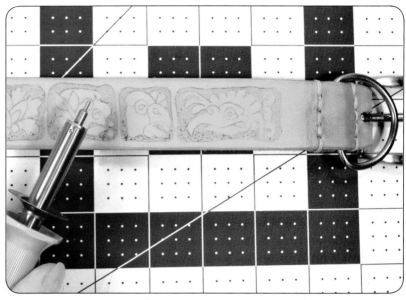

Figure 6.59. Mayan Boot Belt

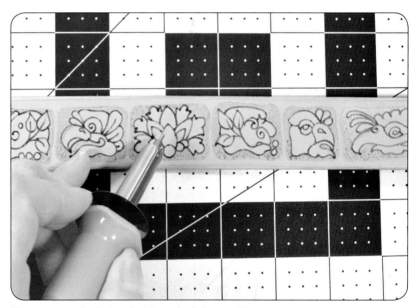

Figure 6.60. Outlining the Hieroglyph Pattern Lines

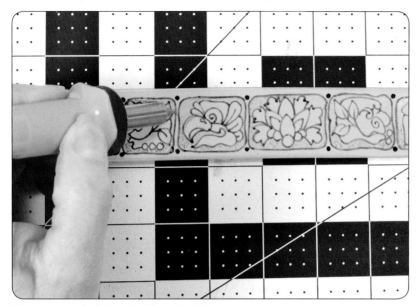

Figure 6.61. Outlining the Hieroglyph Squares

5. Outline the squares around each hieroglyph. Allow the outlining to have a few curves, rounded edges, and indents to create the impression of stone cuts. Lift the tool into an upright position so that the tool body is at a 90-degree angle to the leather. Touch the tip to the leather; then lift the tip straight off the leather to burn the medium-sized black spots between each square. Use this same touch-and-lift stroke to fill in the eyes of your hieroglyph characters (see Fig. 6.61).

6. Use a document cleaning pad, synthetic all-purpose eraser, or white artist's eraser to remove any tracing lines or pencil marks on your finished boot belt. Remove the erasing dust with a dry, lint-free cloth. Brush two to three light coats of satin acrylic leather sealer to the vegetable-tanned side of your belt.

NOTE: The boot belt patterns in this book can easily be adjusted to fit your boot size. Each pattern has a 1" (25mm) repeat pattern that is used in the latch-hole end of the belt. Simply add or subtract these repeat patterns to resize your belt.

Figure 6.62. Mayan Boot Belt (Pattern is shown on page 101.)

Figure 6.63. The North American Indian Boot Belt is worked on a 22½" (572mm) long x 1½" (38mm) wide belt blank, which includes the 2½" (63.5mm) buckle fold; it is cut from 6/7-ounce leather. The steel buckle measures 1¾" (44.5mm) long x 2" (51mm) long and has a 1½" (38mm) latch bar. The large solid-fill areas are filled with tightly packed touch-and-lift dots. (Pattern is shown on page 101.)

Figure 6.64. For the Oriental Dragon Boot Belt, use 6/7-ounce leather cut to 21½" (533mm) long x 1½" (38mm) wide, which includes the 2½" (63.5mm) fold. The buckle measures 2" (51mm) wide x 1¼" (32mm) long, with a latch bar measuring 1½" (38mm). The dragon design is a simple outline burn. The pale-toned background was worked by letting the pyrography tool cool and then working a tightly packed scrubbie stroke as the tip reheated. (Pattern is shown on page 102.)

NOTE: The pattern for the Feathered Wristband needed a 2" (51mm) wide by 6" (152mm) long area on the leather, but the buckle I wanted to use had a latch bar measurement of only 1½" (38mm) wide. I first cut the wristband blank to measure 14½" (369mm) long—12" (305mm) for the body of the band and a 2½" (63.5mm) fold to secure the buckle. With a pencil and ruler, working on the raw side of the leather, I marked a cutting guideline ¼" (6mm) along both long sides of the blank. Using a dime as a tracing template, I marked a small arc where the blank needed to decrease in size—from the buckle latch hole to the end of the fold area—and to allow 4" (102mm) for the end holes. Once the blank had been reduced to accommodate the buckle bar size, I continued the general belt construction. The feather pattern was burned using a micro-ball tip, outlining all of the pattern tracing lines. Thinned acrylic paints added a touch of red to the bead strings, yellow to the beads, and white to the top fluff feather barbs.

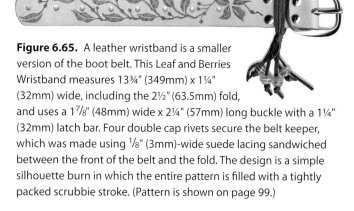

Figure 6.65. A leather wristband is a smaller version of the boot belt. This Leaf and Berries Wristband measures 13¾" (349mm) x 1¼" (32mm) wide, including the 2½" (63.5mm) fold, and uses a 1⅞" (48mm) wide x 2¼" (57mm) long buckle with a 1¼" (32mm) latch bar. Four double cap rivets secure the belt keeper, which was made using ⅛" (3mm)-wide suede lacing sandwiched between the front of the belt and the fold. The design is a simple silhouette burn in which the entire pattern is filled with a tightly packed scrubbie stroke. (Pattern is shown on page 99.)

Figure 6.66. Feathered Wristband. (Pattern is shown on page 121.)

CHAPTER 7
Pyrography Practice Board

Pyrography Practice Board projects are intended to let you just play with your pyrography tool and tips, as well as learn how they work on your leather pieces. These projects do not require total control over your lines or careful shading for realistic patterns. As you work through the Practice Board Journal, you will discover that all of the tonal-value squares are simply doodle patterns that you have made many times over on a scrap of paper—but this time you are putting these doodles to work on leather.

I work a small practice piece before I begin a new project—this gives me a chance to create enough lines and textures so that my hand becomes relaxed during the work. The practice board often sits beside my main project, even if it is nothing more than a scrap of leather, so that I can test a shading stroke, temperature settings, or which pen tip I want to use for the main project.

Tonal Values and Fill Patterns

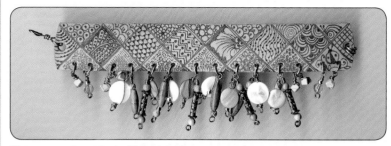

Figure 7.1. Practice Grid Wristband

This simple copper wire-latched wristband uses a variety of line and fill patterns that you can work to create tonal values and fill textures. The band is cut from 6/7 oz. vegetable-tanned leather; it measures 7¼" (184mm) long x 1⅛" (28.5mm) wide. A ¼" (6mm) hole is punched at each end of the leather band for the 18-gauge copper-wire split ring and latch hook. A series of ⅛" (3mm) holes are punched along one long edge of the leather band for the addition of the bent-wire jewelry bead dangles.

A ¾" (19mm) x ¾" (19mm) grid is created and traced onto the leather in a diagonal, diamond-shaped position using graphite tracing paper. Using the one-temperature pyrography burner and the medium ball tip, each diamond is filled with a different line pattern, or texture fill. After the burning is complete, apply one to three thin coats of acrylic leather finisher, allowing each coat to dry completely before beginning the next. Add your jewelry bead accents—created using 18-gauge and 22-gauge wire and a variety of 4- to 8-mm glass beads—to the wristband with copper jump rings. For large-sized wristbands, increase the length of the leather band by 1" inch (25mm). This increases the pattern grid by one full diamond shape. Pattern is shown on page 99.

Scrap Bag Hair Clip

I find that after cutting my leather projects, I have a pile of scraps that may be too small for a belt, purse, or journal project, but too large to throw away. After several projects, I gather up my scraps and spend a little time cutting them into key tags, wristbands, hair barrettes, and even pockets that can be added to future projects. Then I dress out the edges with my edge beveler, Gum Tragacanth, and edge slicker. I keep these small projects in a box next to my pyrography kit, ready to become a Practice Board for the larger project that I am working on. The Practice Board Wristband is one of those creations. It is my Practice Board that I used to work out the textures and pattern fills, tonal-value heat settings, and pen-tip profiles that we will be using in the Practice Board Journal.

When I began the work on the Henna Key Tags, shown on page 10, I was not sure how I wanted to work the different layers of petals in the flower design. So I grabbed an older piece of leather from my scrap bag and did a test burning of a few texture- and line-shading patterns and a sample portion of a henna pattern. When the Henna Key Tags were finished and I was cleaning my work table, I picked up that test scrap—I was about to throw it away. Instead, I got out my cutting knife and rotary punch and turned that scrap into this 4½" (115mm) x 2" (51mm) Scrap Bag Hair Clip (see Fig. 7.2). I even cut the texture test-burn area into tiny triangles, which I added to copper wire with the bead accents. (See pattern, p. 121.)

Figure 7.2 . The Scrap Bag Hair Clip was worked out of a 4¼" (108mm) x 1¼" (32mm) leftover cut from 6/7-ounce leather. The small leather accents were cut from the scrap that I used as my practice board piece for another full project. Instead of throwing away that little bit of pyrography leather, I cut it into small triangles and added those pieces to my hair barrette, along with the bead dangles.

Wild Rose and Practice Board Journal

Figure 7.3 Wild Rose and Practice Board Journal

Supplies

See Basic Supply Lists, p. v

◇ Pyrography pen tips—medium writing tip, wide ball tip

◇ Pyrography tip-cleaning supplies

◇ 6/7-ounce vegetable-tanned leather
  1—10¼" (260mm) x 7¼" (184mm) for journal cover
  2—7¼" (184mm) x 3¾" (96mm) for inner pockets
  2—7¼" (184mm) x 3¼" (83mm) for outer pockets

◇ 2 yards of ⅛" (3mm) suede lacing

◇ ³⁄₁₆" (5mm) or ¼" (6mm) round drive punch

◇ Waxed linen thread

◇ 2 Harness or tapestry needles

◇ 6" (152mm) ceramic bowl or plate

◇ Kitchen snack bag clips

This project will enable you to experiment, practice, and discover how your pyrography tool performs, as well as to identify what type of line or shading each pen tip creates, including a few of the texture and line patterns that can be used to fill or shade an area of your design. The leathercrafting steps can be used with any of the journal, diary, or pocket folder projects in the book. During the burning of the grid-work squares, you will create the varying shades of sepia brown that are used to define tonal values, and then use them in the background and shading of the Wild Rose pattern.

Leathercrafting Instructions

You can work the pyrography steps for your project onto the cut piece before you do the leather construction steps, or you can wait until the construction is complete and then burn the image. If I am working on a leather construction project, such as a new tote pattern or belt pocket pattern, for the first time, I often wait until the leathercrafting steps are complete before I burn. This way, if I make mistakes or need to adjust any of the pieces, I can do so without being concerned that I am cutting into the pyrography pattern. If I have worked the leather pattern several times, I will do the burning before I begin the hole cutting or stitching steps.

1 Using a craft knife, rotary cutter, or bench knife, cut one journal cover and two inner pockets from your 6/7-ounce vegetable-tanned leather. Cut one inner pocket. Reverse the inner pocket by turning it face down onto the leather, and cut one mirror-image inner pocket (*see Figs. 7.4 and 7.5*).

2 Skiver the edges of the leather pieces. Work each tanned side edge using the edge beveler. Coat each edge with Gum Tragacanth and burnish the damp edges using a wooden-edged slicker.

3 With a soft #6 pencil, mark a stitching line ¼" (6mm) from the outer edge of the journal cover. Starting at one corner, make a pencil mark every ¼" (6mm) for each stitching hole. Lay the journal cover on a thick cork board or poly board; use an awl to cut each hole.

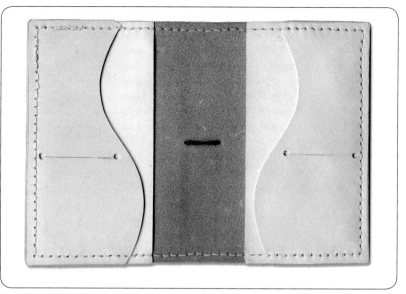

Figure 7.4. Practice Journal—Interior View

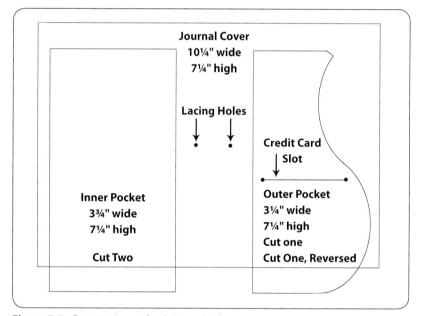

Figure 7.5. Practice Journal—Cutting Guide

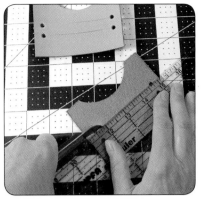

Figure 7.6. End Holes for a Credit Card Slot

Figure 7.7. Cutting the Credit Card Slot

Punching a hole at each end of a credit card slot gives the slot more flexibility when a card is slid inside it. The photos shown above are for a belt purse and are not used for the Practice Board Journal project.

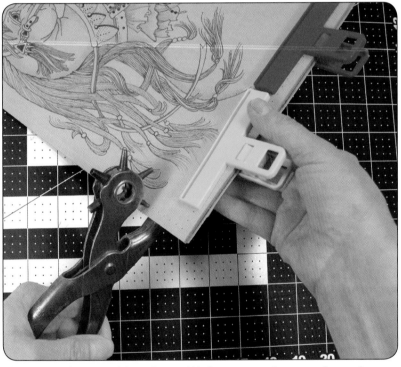

Figure 7.8. Plastic snack bag clips and kitchen storage clamps can be used to hold several layers of leather as you mark and cut holes, or as you stitch. Because these clamps have a light pressure spring, they do not damage the leather. Heavy-duty clamps can be used by placing scrap leather between the clamp and the project piece.

4. With the rotary punch, punch the credit card slot holes in the two inner pockets. Using a craft knife, work along the edge of a metal ruler, cutting a line between the two credit card slot holes (see Figs. 7.6 and 7.7).

5. With a soft #6 pencil, mark a stitching line ¼" (6mm) from the top, bottom, and outer edges of all four pockets. Starting at one corner, make a pencil mark every ¼" (6mm) for each stitching hole. Lay the pockets, working one at a time, on a thick cork board or poly board and use an awl to punch each stitching hole.

6. Position the inner and outer pockets on the inside of the journal cover. Hold in place using removable spray adhesive and bag clips (see Figs. 7.8 and 7.9).

7. Cut a 2-yard length of waxed linen thread. Thread one harness needle on each end of the thread. Using a double-needle stitch, stitch along the journal cover, securing the inner and outer pockets to the cover. Add new lengths of thread as needed. Clean and remove any pencil marks using a synthetic all-purpose eraser.

8. Using a ³⁄₁₆" (5mm) round drive punch, create the lacing holes in the center of the journal cover. Adjust the placement of the holes to match the grid lines on your journal so that each hole falls on the most central grid-work vertical line at the top or bottom of a grid square.

9 When the pyrography work is done, lightly dampen the center line on the inside of the journal cover. Gently fold the cover until the two outer edges of the cover touch. Allow the damp leather to dry overnight before adding any finish.

10 Using a ³/₁₆" (5mm) round drive punch, make two holes in the center spine area of your journal in which to thread the suede lacing tie. Center the holes to the journal cover, positioning them so that each hole falls on an intersection of one of the grid squares.

11 Cut an 18" (457mm) length of ¹/₈" (3mm) suede lacing. Thread the lacing through the two lacing holes at the center of the journal cover. Tie an overhand knot in both sides of the lacing, as close to the cover holes as possible. Bring the lacings to the side edges of the journal and tie in a simple bow to hold the journal cover closed.

Using Spray Adhesive

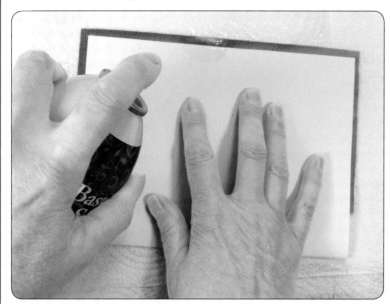

Figure 7.9. Using Spray Adhesive

Removable spray adhesive can be used to temporarily hold two pieces of leather together during the hole punching, awl work, and stitching. Cover your work area with paper towels. Cut a piece of paper ¼" (6mm) shorter than each edge of the piece to be secured. Center the paper over the leather to protect all areas that do not need spray adhesive. Follow the directions for use on the can and spray one coat of adhesive along the exposed edges. Place the leather piece onto the main leather piece and press into place. When your hole cutting or stitching is complete, you can remove any exposed adhesive using an all-purpose synthetic eraser.

Figure 7.10. Graphite paper leaves a thin, medium-gray line on your leather. That line can be removed after the burning is complete using either a document cleaning pad or a synthetic all-purpose eraser.

Figure 7.11. Tracing the Pattern

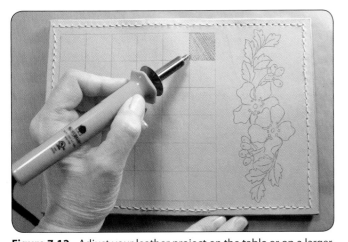

Figure 7.12. Adjust your leather project on the table or on a larger plywood board in your lap to allow as comfortable a hand position as possible while burning. I have a 14" (356mm)-square x ½" (13mm)-thick plywood board that I often use to support my leather as I work. I can rest one edge of the board against the edge of my craft table. The opposite edge of the plywood board rests against my legs. This slants the work nicely for me and allows me to work for several hours at a time.

Pyrography Instructions

1 Copy the Wild Rose pattern onto a piece of tracing paper or semi-transparent vellum. Set it aside for the moment. With a ruler and a soft #6–#8, pencil, create a grid pattern on your journal cover using 1" (25mm) squares. The top, bottom, and back-edge lines of the grid are worked ⅝" (16mm) from the leather edge to the center of the grid. Extend the top and bottom lines of the grid onto the front side of the journal cover. Connect these two lines with a pencil line marked ⅝" (16mm) from the front edge. (See pattern, p. 109.)

NOTE: Leathercrafting carving techniques often call for you to dampen the leather and then trace a pattern to create a fine indented line in the surface of the leather. For leather pyrography you will want to avoid any step that will create an indented line because the tip of your burning pen will skip or slip as you pull your stroke over that line. Graphite paper allows you to transfer the pattern onto dry leather without creating indented lines in the surface *(see Fig. 7.10).*

2 Center the Wild Rose pattern into the large, pencil-line rectangle on the front cover of your journal. Using graphite paper, trace the pattern outlines. For most patterns you will not need to trace all of the fine detailing lines. These can be worked by hand as you develop your burning *(see Fig. 7.11).*

3 Using a low-range, one-temperature pyrography tool and the medium writing tip or medium ball tip, burn a diagonal line from the left top corner to the right bottom corner of the top row, farthest right square. Leaving a thin amount of unburned space between the lines, fill the remaining areas of the square with diagonal lines that follow the path of the first line. This creates one layer of cross-hatched line work. Because this square is now half-filled with thin burned lines and half-filled with thin, unburned stripes, the square takes on a pale-medium tonal value *(see Fig. 7.12).*

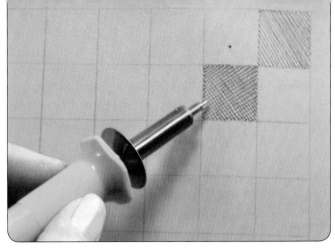

Figure 7.13. Cross-hatching is worked by burning multiple layers of tightly packed parallel lines, changing the directional slant of the lines with each new layer. Without changing the tip size, temperature setting, or the time used to make each stroke, you can deepen the tonal value of an area by working a new layer of burned lines over the previous work.

Work the second square along the diagonal of your grid work with two layers of parallel lines. Work the first layer in the same directional slant as you worked square one. Work the second layer in the opposite direction. Because you have now worked twice as many burned lines in the second square than in the first, the second square takes on a deeper tonal value (see Fig. 7.13).

Work through each grid-work square, adding one new layer of cross-hatching with each new square than you used in the previous square. The bottom right-hand square will have six layers of cross-hatched lines. A standard repeat formula for cross-hatching is to work on the left diagonal, on the right diagonal, vertical, horizontal, and then repeat the pattern (see Fig. 7.14).

NOTE: When this row is finished, the first square will have a pale-medium tone. By the time you have worked all of the layers into the sixth square, few or no unburned areas remain. This square has an even, deep-brown coloration and is the darkest tonal value. The completed line of six grid-work squares creates a tonal value scale, also called a sepia scale, worked from the palest value to the darkest.

Figure 7.14 . With each layer of new work you add, the deeper the tonal value becomes.

The second row of diagonal squares is worked by simply touching, then lifting, the tip of your medium-ball-tip pen or your medium writing tip pen, creating very small dots. If the tip is allowed to rest for a brief moment on the leather, the dot will be slightly larger and darker than those that are worked with a quick touch. Begin by filling one-half of the area in the top square with both pale and dark spots. With each new square add more dots. This touch-and-lift dot pattern is often used to completely fill an area of your pattern with black tonal values (see Fig. 7.15).

Figure 7.15. The second diagonal line of grid-work squares is worked using only a small touch-and-lift dot.

Fill about one half of the space in the first square on the next diagonal line of squares with small, over-lapping circles or coils. Touch the tip of your pen to the leather and begin making tight circular motions as if you were tracing along a stretched spring. Work at keeping all of the circles approximately the same size. Work through the next three squares in the diagonal line, adding a new layer of overlapping circles in each square (see Fig. 7.16).

Figure 7.16. The next diagonal row of sepia shading is created using small circles and ovals that overlap each other. Those circles are worked as one connecting line, similar to an uncoiled spring.

Figure 7.17. The scrubbie stroke is done with a steady, slow movement across the leather, creating a curved, circular, or random patterned line. The straight-line fill-stroke is worked in a back-and-forth, or up-and-down, motion that fills the center of your square with straight lines.

Figure 7.18. Solid-Line Shading

Unplug your pyrography tool and allow it to cool. Remove the medium writing tip and replace it with the wide-ball tip. The wide-ball burns slightly thicker lines that will be used in these next few texture-fill squares.

NOTE: The scrubbie stroke, worked into the diagonal row to the left of the cross-hatch row—also called the random doodle stroke—is a meandering line that twists, turns, and curls (see Fig. 7.17). There is no set direction or path for the curved line. Fill the first square in the third diagonal line with the scrubbie stroke, allowing about one-third to one-half of the area to remain unburned. These unburned areas will be the spaces captured inside of your coiled circles. With each new square, add a new layer of scrubbie stroke. The fifth square will have five layers of scrubbie strokes burned. The last square will have a solid texture-fill dark value, but it will also have a slight mottling to the tonal value. This is my favorite shading stroke because the mottling adds a little extra dimension to an otherwise solid-fill area.

The straight-line stroke is excellent for creating animal and human hair, as well as to create the impression of a distant line of trees in the deep background of a landscape. Move the pen tip in an up-and-down motion, reversing your direction each time you reach the edge of the square. One square will be filled with just one or two lines that continually turn at the top and bottom of the square. Continue working this texture pattern through each square in the diagonal row; add one new layer of strokes with each new square.

Unplug your pyrography tool and allow it to cool completely. Remove the medium writing tip and install your flat-shader tip into the pen. Re-plug the pyrography tool, and begin working this step as the tool begins to heat, but has not yet reached its full temperature. In the next diagonal row, left of the scrubbie stroke row, lay the wide, flat side of the shader tip against one side of the edge of the top square and pull a straight horizontal line to touch the opposite edge of the square. Repeat the line stroke, starting in the same position, touching the stroke you just made. Continue until the square is filled with wide, long, touching lines. Work the second diagonal square with one full layer of horizontal lines, and then turn your tool tip to burn a layer of vertical lines. The third diagonal square receives one layer of horizontal lines, one layer of vertical lines, and one layer of horizontal lines. Since we have worked only three layers of flat shader lines into the third square, that square gives the impression of woven fabric or basket weaving. When you add more layers, the flat shader will create even, solid-black tones.

10 The last three upper squares on the left are filled with fine-line designs. Unplug your pyrography tool and allow it to cool completely. Since we have been burning for about one hour and have worked over one hundred layers of burned lines, take a few moments and clean your tips on your leather strop and honing compound. Remove the flat shader tip and install your micro-writing tip into the pen. Re-plug the pyrography tool, and when it reaches its full temperature setting, work the fine-line designs shown in the top right-hand three squares.

11 The remaining six grid-work squares are worked in circular patterns burned with the micro-ball tip. One square is worked to look like dragon scales, the next like different small stones closely packed together, the third uses tightly packed, small spirals, and another becomes an ever-widening spiral. These squares use only one layer of burning and are fun background fill designs for any pattern work *(see Fig. 7.20)*.

12 Once your grid-work squares are filled, take a moment to look at your burning as one piece or pattern, instead of separate little squares. You can see that using a one-temperature pyrography pen and three pen tips, you have total control over the tonal value of your work. Your finished grid should have several extremely pale-toned squares, some light mid-tones, some dark mid-tones, and a few very dark tones. This range of tonal values is what pyrographers use to create detailed shaded drawing *(see Fig. 7.21)*.

Figure 7.19 . Texture-fill strokes do not have to be random doodle or curved lines. You can use any line design that is easy to repeat. These squares have only one layer of burning.

Figure 7.20. Continue using the micro-writing pen tip for the remaining practice square. Small designs can be used as texture-fills. In our Practice Board Journal one square is filled with a multi-petaled flower.

Figure 7.21. Completed Practice Square Grid-Work

Figure 7.22. You will be using the tonal values that you created in the grid-work squares to work a detailed drawing for a sprig of wild roses. Before you begin burning the background texture scrubbie strokes, divide the full Wild Rose design visually into four quarters. The first layer of this work will be worked over the entire background. Each new layer will be reduced by one left-side quarter of the background to create the graduation from left to right.

Figure 7.23. Often, you only need a small amount of shading inside of the elements of your pattern to create a realistic look to your work.

13 Using a low-range, one-temperature pyrography pen and the medium writing or ball tip, work the Wild Rose design in a tightly packed scrubbie stroke to the entire background (see Fig. 7.22). Work three more layers of scrubbie stroke, reducing the amount of space you fill by one-quarter of the width of the Wild Rose design area with each new layer. Work one more ¼"(6mm)-wide layer along the right side edge of the rectangle. You should have a graduated shaded background with its palest area in the lower right-hand corner, and the darkest values in the upper right-hand corner and along the outer edge of the pattern area.

14 Using a series of tightly packed parallel lines and the medium writing tip or ball tip, shade one-half of each leaf, working from the center vein line toward the outer edge of the leaf. On a few of the Wild Rose petals, work parallel-line shading from the outer edge of the petal toward the flower center. Curve each fine-line stroke to match the closest edge of the flower petal (see Fig. 7.23).

15 Outline the traced pattern lines. Referring to the original pattern, add the detail lines shown in the veining of the leaves, inside the petals, and the flower center. This completes the steps to burning the Wild Rose portion of this pattern (see Fig. 7.24).

Figure 7.24. Outlining the pattern lines of a design separates the pattern elements from the background shading.

Figure 7.25. To move this work from a practice board into a finished art-style design, you can cut circular lines using a craft knife and a ceramic plate as a cutting guide.

16 To add a little surprise or unexpected tension into the design work, I used an 8" (203mm) ceramic plate as a cutting template for my craft knife. These knife cuts are worked in two separate cutting strokes. Lay the plate face down on your leather journal cover. For the first stroke, place your knife at a slight angle away from the plate onto the leather and cut a line about 1/16" (2mm) deep into the leather surface *(see Fig. 7.25)*.

17 Set your knife back into the cut line, but this time slant the knife blade away from the cut line. Pull a cutting stroke to remove a small v-shaped piece of leather from the journal's surface. If you wish to use a knife cut line or knife-scraped area in your designs, keep the deepest part of the v-shaped cut less than one-half the thickness of your leather to avoid excessively weakening it *(see Fig. 7.26)*.

18 To remove dirt and any remaining pattern-tracing lines, use a document cleaning pad, a synthetic all-purpose eraser, or a white artist's eraser. Work the entire surface to insure that every area is cleaned. Remove the cleaning dust with a dry, lint-free cloth *(see Fig. 7.27)*.

19 Brush two to three light coats of satin acrylic leather finisher to the cover and tanned leather sides of the inside pockets. Let each coat dry completely before applying the next.

Figure 7.26. Cutting the leather reveals that the inside area—the leather below the tanned surface—is much whiter or paler in tonal value than the vegetable-tanned surface. This adds one more tonal value to your sepia range in your pyrography work.

Figure 7.27. Pyrography media will collect a small amount of dirt and oil from your hands and from the work surface. A document cleaning pad is shown in this photo. It is a cotton-linen cloth bag that is filled with finely ground eraser particles.

Figure 7.28. A pattern layout with the large grid-work area bordered by a smaller rectangular design field can be used over and over again to experiment with new fill patterns, new texture strokes, and small pieces of larger, realistic designs.

CHAPTER 8

Pyrography Projects

This project chapter begins with two simple outlined and lightly shaded patterns, worked on common leather items, and continues with fine details and shading; adding multiple layers of leather; experimenting with darker tonal values and texture shading; bringing color into your projects; and working through a full-range, sepia tonal-value burning. Leather allows you to create usable items such as journals, purses, and key tags. Review the project steps to better understand the workflow.

Carousel Horse Book Cover — *Simple Outlining*

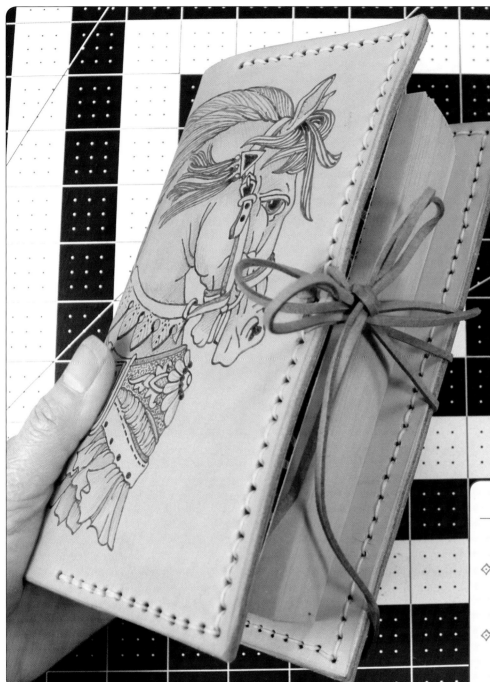

The first project, the Carousel Horse Book Cover, begins with leathercrafting techniques, moves on to pyrography involving two burning strokes—fine line and touch-and-lift dots—and then finishes with leather construction.

Supplies

See Basic Supply Lists, p. v

- ❖ Pyrography pen tips — medium writing tip or ball tip, micro writing tip
- ❖ 6/7 ounce vegetable-tanned leather
  1—11¼" (285mm) x 8" (285mm) for journal cover
  2—8" (285mm) by 4½" (115mm) for inner pockets
- ❖ 2 yards of ⅛" (3mm) suede lacing
- ❖ Waxed linen thread
- ❖ 2 Harness or tapestry needles
- ❖ Kitchen bag clips

Leathercrafting Instructions

Refer to the general leathercrafting instructions on pages 47–49.

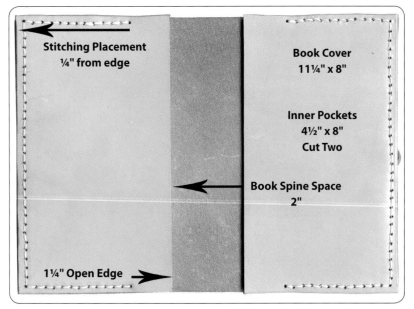

Figure 8.1. Cutting

Stitching Placement
¼" from edge

Book Cover
11¼" x 8"

Inner Pockets
4½" x 8"
Cut Two

Book Spine Space
2"

1¼" Open Edge

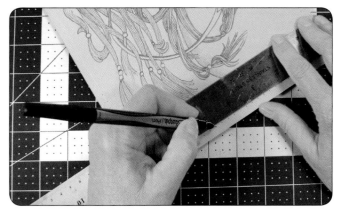

Figure 8.2. Marking the Stitching-Hole Placement

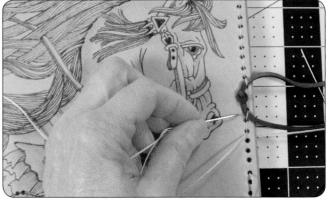

Figure 8.3. Securing the Suede Lacings

1 Work the pyrography steps for this project before you do the leather-crafting for the stitching.

2 Cut one book cover and two inner pockets from 6/7-ounce leather. Trim the edges using the edge beveler *(see Fig. 8.1)*.

3 Use the skiver to thin the three outer edges of the two inner pockets.

4 Mark your stitching-hole placement using a #6–#8 pencil *(see Fig. 8.2)*. The stitches lie ¼" (6mm) in from the outer edge of the book cover and are spaced ¼" (6mm) apart. Along the top and bottom edges of the book cover the stitching runs 3¼" (83mm) from the front or back edge of the cover. This leaves a 1¼" (32mm) space of unstitched leather on both of the inner pockets on the inside edge, which gives extra room to safely and easily insert the covers of your favorite paperback.

5 Cut the suede lacing into two 1-yard lengths. Tie an overhand knot in the center of each lacing.

6 With waxed thread and two harness needles, double-needle stitch the inner pockets to the book cover. As you work the front-edge stitching, lay one suede lacing over the cover at the center point stitch hole. Work your double-needle stitching over the suede lacing one stitch before the center stitch hole. Work the center stitch hole. Then work the stitching over the suede lacing one stitch after the center stitch hole. Repeat this process to secure the back lacing to the cover *(see Fig. 8.3)*.

When the burning is complete, using Gum Tragacanth and the edge beveler, smooth all of the outer edges of your book cover. Allow the cover to dry completely.

 Brush two or three light coats of satin acrylic finish on your project to seal the leather.

Pyrography Instructions

This Carousel Horse pattern uses just two burning strokes—the fine-line stroke and the touch-and-lift dot. To create the mid-sized outlines we will use the medium writing tip or ball-tip pen. For the fine-line shading, change out the pen tip to the micro-writing tip. The sample for this project was burned using the low-range, one-temperature burning pen.

 Using graphite paper, trace the pattern *(see page 122)* to your pre-cut leather book cover, centering the pattern to the leather.

 Plug your low-range one-temperature burning tool into your surge protector. Allow the pen tip to reach its full heat. Work a line stroke along all of the main pattern outlines. Note: In Figure 8.5, I have only traced those basic outlines during the tracing step. The smaller detail lines in the pattern can be worked free-hand. (See pattern, p. 122.)

 Unplug your low-range, one-temperature tool and allow it to cool completely. Exchange the medium tip for the micro-writing tip. Re-plug and reheat your burning tool and allow it to reach its full temperature setting. Work one layer of fine parallel-line shading to the horse's face, where it lies under the bridle leather, and along the front edge of the neck. Work a two-layer cross-hatching along the horse's body where it touches the mane, bridle, chest harness, and along the back.

Figure 8.4. Tracing the Pattern

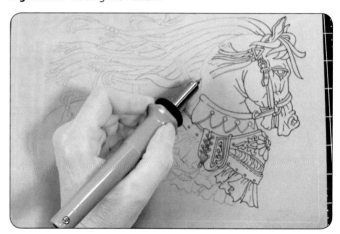

Figure 8.5. Outlining Using the Medium Writing Tip

Figure 8.6. Fine-Line Shading

> ✎ **TIP** ✎ Because I am an avid pyrographer, I have two low-range, one-temperature pyrography tools that I can set up with my surge protector at the same time. This allows me to have two different pen tips hot and ready for use at any point during the burning steps. I also have a scrap of leather on my work table to do quick text burns and to experiment with shading techniques. When I move from one pyrography tool to the other, I work several quick lines of burn with the second tool on my scrap leather. This releases the heat that has built up on the tip while it was not in use.

Figure 8.7. Line-Fill the Mane

4 Using the medium writing tip or ball tip, fill the wide strands of mane with hair lines that flow with the curve of each area. Allow some lines to "disappear" by bringing them to touch the outline. Allow some lines to tuck under other lines.

5 Using either the medium writing tip, ball tip, or the micro-writing tip, shade the bridle with fine lines that begin at the top of each section and flow down towards the bottom section of each piece.

6 With the medium writing tip or ball tip, work the solid-fill shading in the harness and bridle. Fill the pupil of the horse's eye with a solid-fill black value. The black tones are created by working over the line stroke several times, adding multiple dark layers to the area, or by using the touch-and-lift dot fill and densely packing the dots to completely fill the area.

7 Remove any remaining graphite paper or pencil tracing lines using a document cleaning pad or synthetic all-purpose eraser. Remove the eraser dust with a dry, lint-free cloth.

8 The pyrography steps are complete, and your project is ready to move back into the leather construction steps (see pages 58–59).

Figure 8.8. Shading the Bridle Fabric

Figure 8.9. Solid Fill Shading in the Harness and Bridle

NOTE: This project can be easily adapted to fit a favorite book. Measure the dimensions of the book that you want to protect with a leather cover. Add 1" (25mm) to the height measurement to allow room for the stitching. Add 1½" (38mm) to the width measurement to allow for stitching and room for the leather to bend around the book in the center section of the cover. For paperback books, keep the top and bottom stitching along the inner pockets to ½ to ¾ of the width of the paperback book cover. For hardcover books, keep the stitching along the top and bottom edges of the inner pockets to ¼ the width of the book cover.

Steampunk Dragon Purse — *Simple Outlining and Simple Background Fill*

This Steampunk Dragon Purse pattern is worked using a rheostat-controlled tool and the medium writing or ball-tip pen.

Supplies

See Basic Supply Lists, p. v

- ◇ Rheostat-controlled or variable-temperature Burning Unit
- ◇ Pyrography pens—medium writing or ball-tip pen
- ◇ 1—14¾" (375mm) x 8¼" (209mm), 6/7-ounce leather for the purse flap and back
- ◇ 1—6¼" (165mm) x 8¼" (209mm), 6/7-ounce leather for the purse front
- ◇ 1—17" (432mm) x 1¾" (44.5mm), 6/7-ounce leather for center purse strip
- ◇ 2—¾" (19mm) x 3" (77mm), 6/7-ounce leather for the dee ring side straps
- ◇ 1—¾" (19mm) x 34" (864mm), 6/7-ounce leather for the shoulder strap
- ◇ 2—¾" (19mm) wide steel dee rings
- ◇ 4—Screw-post rivets

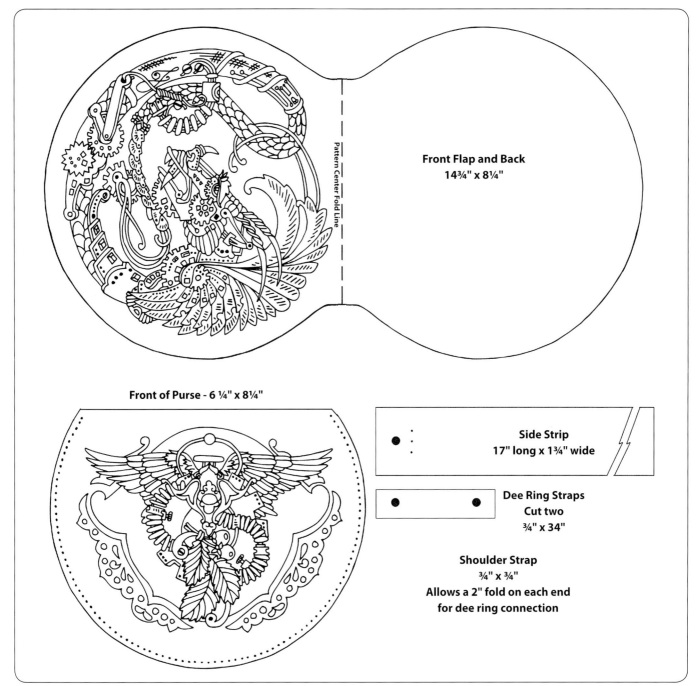

Figure 8.10. Steampunk Dragon Purse

NOTE: This purse has a surprise waiting for its user—the Steampunk Dragon flap covers a second complete pyrography burn of Winged Gears! Only when you open the flap does the inner burning show.

Work the pyrography burning before you move to the leather construction steps. Cut the leather pieces from 6/7-ounce leather. Trace the dragon pattern to the fold-over flap part and the winged gears pattern to the front inside part, using graphite tracing paper. The medium writing or ball-tip pen is used with either a rheostat-controlled or variable-temperature burning unit. Do a test burn on one of the leather scraps left over from the cutting process to establish the temperature setting your unit will use to create a dark-brown line and a pale sienna solid-fill shading. (See patterns, pp. 110–111.)

Leathercrafting Instructions

Refer to the general leathercrafting instructions on pages 47–49, for the Practice Board Journal Cover.

1 Mark your stitching holes ¼" (6mm) from the outer edge of the flap/back, front, and side strip with ³⁄₁₆" (5mm) between each stitch. Use an awl and thick cork board to punch the stitching holes. Use a rotary punch the size of your screw posts to create the post holes in the dee ring straps and the two ends of the shoulder strap. Work the leather edges with the edge beveler and the Gum Tragacanth.

2 Lightly dampen the rawhide side of the side strip with clean water. Allow the dampened strip to sit for a moment or two to soften the leather. Using waxed thread and two harness needles, double-needle stitch the side strip to the flap/back piece. Stitch the side strip to the front piece using the same double-needle stitching. As you work this stitching step you can ease and adjust the side strip into position against the round edges of the front and back of the purse.

3 Fold one dee ring strap in half with the tanned leather side showing. Slide one dee ring into the fold of the strap. Hold the folded strap against the side strip. Slide the long end of a screw post through both layers of the strap and then through the purse side strip. On the inside of the purse attach the second part of the screw post to the long side of the screw post, and tighten. Repeat this step for the second dee ring strap.

4 Slide one end of the shoulder strap through the dee ring on the purse with the short, folded side on the inside of the shoulder strap. Join the strap to the fold with a screw post. Repeat for the second shoulder strap side.

5 Lightly dampen the narrow center area of the flap/back piece with clean water, as in step 2. Roll the flap over the purse front until the two bottom edges meet. Lay your purse, flap down, on a dry terry cloth towel. Place a paperback book on top of the purse to act as a clamp. Let your purse dry overnight.

Figure 8.11. For both the dragon pattern and the winged-gears pattern, outline the traced pattern lines with the medium writing or ball-tip pen. The dark areas in the designs are filled with a touch-and-lift densely packed dot pattern. Small, pale-tone dots are burned by touching the tip to the leather, and then quickly removing the tip from the leather. That quick-touch motion keeps these spots light-colored. Darker spots are burned by allowing just a moment more for the tip to touch the leather.

Figure 8.12. Turn down the temperature setting to the pale sienna tone level. Using the medium writing tip or ball tip and a tightly packed scrubbie stroke, fill in the background space of the pattern to an even, solid fill. Remove any remaining tracing lines with a document cleaning pad or synthetic all-purpose eraser. Remove the eraser dust with a dry, lint-free cloth.

6 To seal your purse from water and dirt, apply two to three light coats of satin acrylic leather finish.

Landscapes, a favorite pyrography pattern motif, are just perfect for this southwestern Desert Landscape Journal. I made this project specifically to hold a weekly diary calendar, appointment cards, and lab slips for my family's medical appointments.

Supplies

See Basic Supply Lists, p. v

◇ Low-range, one-temperature pyrography pen

◇ Medium writing tip or ball tip

◇ 6/7-ounce vegetable-tanned leather

◇ 1—7¼" (184mm) x 10¼" (260mm) Journal cover

◇ 1—3½" (90mm) x 7¼" (184mm) middle left pocket

◇ 1—2½" (63.5mm) x 6¾" (171mm) front left pocket

◇ 1—3½" (90mm) x 7¼" (184mm) middle right pocket

◇ 1—3½" (90mm) x 4" (102mm) front right pocket

◇ 5/6-ounce dark-brown dyed leather

◇ 1—3½" (90mm) x 7¼" (184mm) back left pocket

◇ 1—4¼" (108mm) x 7¼" (184mm) back right pocket

◇ 2 yards ⅛" (3mm) sienna brown suede leather lacing

◇ 1 Screw-post concho

NOTE: The large surface area of a journal, artist's diary, or small notebook leather cover can be treated as one large pattern area or divided into two related pattern areas. In this burning, we will use the entire cover to create one pattern. To balance the visual weight of the front area against the back area of the cover, each contains at least one of the main elements—one tall cactus, one short cactus, one tumbleweed, one mid-ground plateau, and one tall mountain.

> **TIP** I cut and assembled this leather journal before I worked the pyrography pattern. That enabled me to plan in advance where the silver concho and the suede lacing would fall on the leather in relation to the pattern elements. You may find that working the pyrography first, and then assembling the leather, may make handling the leather during the burning steps easier.

Figure 8.13. Desert Landscape Journal, Front

Figure 8.14. Desert Landscape Journal, Back

This multi-layered pocket journal provides lots of pyrography space for a detailed landscape burning.

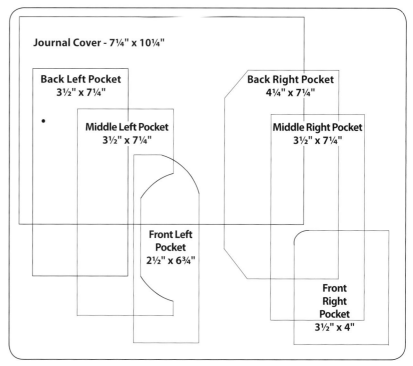

Figure 8.15. Leather Cutting Layout, Desert Landscape Journal

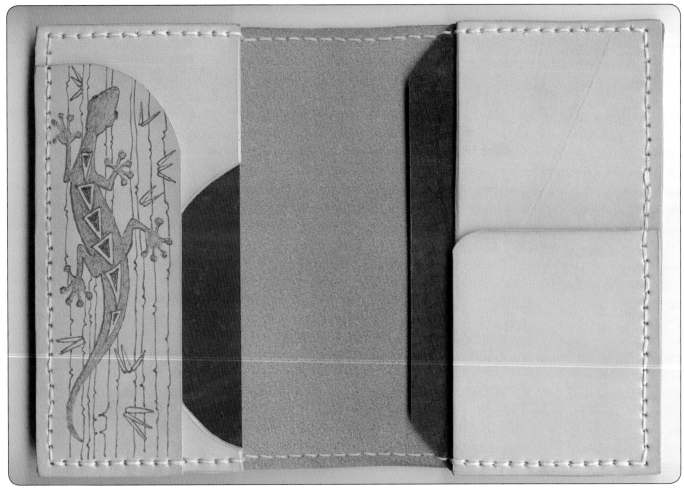

Figure 8.16. Desert Landscape Journal, Inside View

Figure 8.17. As your pyrography skills grow, you will discover that you only need to trace the basic outlines of a pattern, not each and every detail line—traced detail lines can be lost under layers of shading. Most detail lines in your patterns can be worked free-hand during the last steps, or you can spot-trace those detail lines onto the leather after the shading is complete.

1 Following the general leather construction steps for the Practice Board Project in Chapter 7, cut and assemble your leather journal. To add a little extra interest to the inside pocket area of this project, and to balance some of the brown tonal value coloring of the gecko in the leathercrafting, I chose to cut the two back inner pockets from a dark-brown dyed leather. You can mix and match different textures, colors, and weights of leather in your project's construction.

2 Trace your pattern to the journal cover using graphite paper. Trace only those lines that you need to establish the main elements. (See patterns, p. 102 and pp. 118–119.)

With the low-range, one-temperature tool and the medium writing tip or ball tip, work small clusters of short line strokes to the two tumbleweeds. Allow about one-half of the visual space in these tumbleweeds to remain unburned (see Fig. 8.18).

Outline the outer borders of the two tall saguaro cacti. Work long, thin lines through the body and arms of the cactus, following the direction of that part of the cactus. These lines will create the impression of the cactus ribbing. Use small clusters of two to three short line strokes to add the cactus needles (see Fig. 8.19).

Figure 8.18. We have used the short straight-line stroke to add shading to an element and to solid-fill background areas. During this burning, that stroke creates the tumbleweeds in the foreground of the pattern.

Figure 8.19. Outlining the Tall Cactus

Figure 8.20. The prickly pear and yucca fill the foreground of this pattern.

Figure 8.21. Close-Up for Step 5.

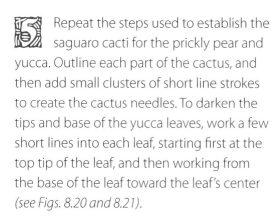

5 Repeat the steps used to establish the saguaro cacti for the prickly pear and yucca. Outline each part of the cactus, and then add small clusters of short line strokes to create the cactus needles. To darken the tips and base of the yucca leaves, work a few short lines into each leaf, starting first at the top tip of the leaf, and then working from the base of the leaf toward the leaf's center *(see Figs. 8.20 and 8.21)*.

6 The light source in this pattern—the sun—is in the upper right-hand corner. The edges of each element nearest the light source will be the brightest area. The edges on the opposite side of the light source will have the darkest shadows. Using a quick motion and a light pressure to keep your shading strokes in the pale tones, work a layer of tightly packed scrubbie stroke to the shadow areas of each cactus and the tumbleweeds *(see Fig. 8.22)*.

Figure 8.22. Determining where your shading should fall is easy once you establish where your light source is in the pattern.

Moving your burning into the mid-ground of this pattern, outline the plateaus, ground lines, and smaller tumbleweeds. Using the same light touch and quick motion as in step 6, work the scrubbie stroke shading to the right-side planes in the plateaus. With a light pressure and quick movements, outline the background mountain range. The light pressure of the writing tip against the leather will burn thinner, paler tonal value lines. Note that in the close-up for step 7, the mountain outlines are very loose doodle lines that curve, twist, and repeat. The farther you are from any landscape element, the less defined or crisply edged that element appears *(see Figs. 8.23 and 8.24)*.

Figure 8.23. The burning strokes that you use for the foreground of your landscapes are repeated in the mid-ground and background areas. Patterns, texture-fills, and line strokes used throughout a pattern unite all of the individual elements in that pattern.

Figure 8.24. Close-Up for Step 7

Figure 8.25. There are some elements in landscape work that you really can't see but need to hint at to make your burning appear realistic. You don't see the sun, water reflections, or wind, but you can imply that they exist by the way you treat the areas affected by these elements. In our landscape, the sun is not burned. Instead, a light line-shading is worked in the surrounding sky space to show where the sun should be.

To suggest that your landscape has a sun just above the mountains, work the surrounding sky area with thin, pale-toned lines that are parallel to the horizon line of the landscape.

Use a document cleaning pad or synthetic all-purpose eraser to remove any dirt or remaining tracing lines from the leather journal cover. Remove the eraser dust with a dry, lint-free cloth. Apply two to three light coats of satin acrylic leather finishing, letting each coat dry thoroughly before working the next.

Flower Garden Lunch Box Purse — *Simple Shading and Solid-Fill Background*

Supplies

See Basic Supply Lists, p. v

◇ Rheostat-controlled or variable-temperature pyrography tool

◇ Medium writing tip or ball tip, wide-ball tip or shading tip

◇ Cork-backed metal ruler

◇ 1—6" (152mm) x 15" (381mm), 5/6-ounce leather for the body

◇ 1—3" (77mm) x 6" (152mm), 5/6-ounce leather for the flap inner pocket

◇ 1—3¼" (83mm) x 6" (152mm), 5/6-ounce leather for the front inner pocket

◇ 2—2" (51mm) x 4" (102mm), 5/6-ounce leather for the sides

◇ 2—5/8" (16mm) x 6" (152mm), 5/6-ounce leather for the strap loops

◇ 2—Double cap rivets

◇ 3—36" (915mm) lengths of 2mm copper chain

◇ 6—8mm copper split rings

◇ 2—1¼" (32mm) copper spring latches

◇ 2—1¼" (32mm) 18-gauge copper-wire bent-wire rings

◇ 12-piece set of artist-quality colored pencils

◇ Satin spray acrylic sealer or reworkable spray sealer

This lunch box is a small, wide purse with a one-piece body that rolls around the side pieces. You will combine the leather construction skills you have learned making the Steampunk Dragon Pill Box Purse, the pyrography skills from the Practice Board Journal, and the colored pencil work from the Pink Petals Key Tag to create this Flower Garden Lunch Box Purse.

Figure 8.26. The basic leathercrafting design of the lunch box purse allows you to cover the entire outside of your purse with pyrography without concern for stitched seam lines.

Leathercrafting Instructions

1 Cut the purse pieces from 5/6-ounce vegetable-tanned leather. This lightweight leather rolls easily into the tight curves at the top and bottom of the purse design. I used an 8" ceramic plate for the cutting template for the curved front edge of the purse body.

> **~ TIP ~** It is easier to work the pyrography steps for this project before you do the construction steps of the leathercrafting. You will cut the leather pieces and then measure, mark, and punch the stitching holes. Next, you will move to the pyrography work. When the burning is completed, you will return to the final construction of this lunch box purse. To keep the leather construction steps together in one place, the cutting steps are steps 1–4. Steps 5–8 are worked *after* the burning.

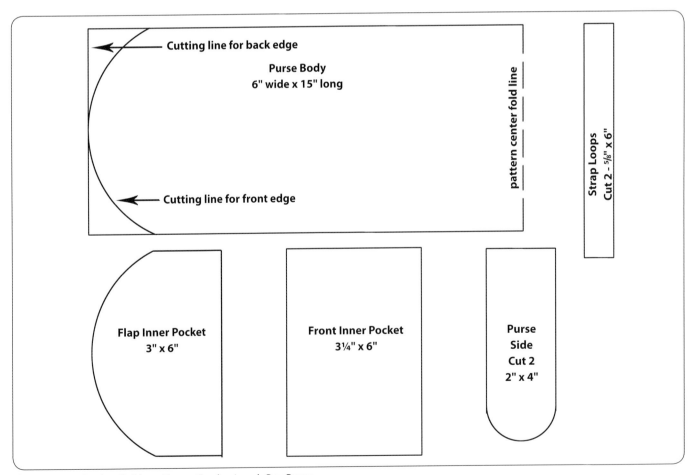

Figure 8.27. Cutting Guide to Flower Garden Lunch Box Purse

NOTE: First, cut the body in a large rectangle measuring 6" (152mm) x 15" (381mm) and then cut the two inner pocket rectangles. Place the body piece on a grid-work cutting mat, adjusted to match the grid lines. Lay one inner pocket over the front edge of the body piece with the tanned side against the mat. Next, place a ceramic plate over one end of the body piece and adjust the plate to match the front center point measurement of the body as well as the sides along one vertical grid line. Hold the plate in place and glide the cutting knife along the plate edge, cutting through both layers of leather. Trim the edges of your cut pieces with the edge beveler and then dress out the edges with Gum Tragacanth and your edge slicker.

2 Measure ¼" (6mm) in from the edges of the body and side piece. This is your stitching line guide. Mark your stitching holes ¼" (6mm) apart on the long sides of the body. Measure the front curve of the body to find the center point of the curve; mark this point with your pencil. Work your ¼" (6mm) stitching holes from this point, working first toward one long side of the purse and then returning to the center point to mark the second half of the curve.

Measure and mark a line 3" (77mm) down into the body from the straight front edge of the body. Mark the center measurement point of this line with a pencil. Working from this center point and toward the outer edge of the body, mark the line in ¼" (6mm) intervals for stitching holes. This stitching line secures the bottom edge of the front inner pocket to the body.

3 As you work the hole-punching steps you can make your stitching holes align by placing the inner pockets under the front, or flap, of the body with the rawhide sides facing and then punch through both layers of leather. Working with a hand awl and a thick cork board or poly board, punch your stitching holes.

4 Cut and mark the stitching holes for the side pieces of the purse, working ¼" (6mm) from the edge of the sides and at ¼" (6mm) intervals. Punch the holes using the hand awl on a thick cork board. With your rotary punch set to the size of the screw posts, create one

hole 1" (25mm) from the top edge of each side. With the rotary punch, create the strap loop holes in the end of both sides of the strap. These holes are 1" (25m) from the end of the strap and centered in the strap.

5 When the pyrography steps for this project are done, complete the leather construction. Using waxed linen thread and harness needles, work the double-needle stitch throughout the project. Begin at one top corner of the front and inner front pocket. Stitch along the entire straight side of the body; end at the curve of the front flap, but do not cut the threads. Work the second side of the purse in the same manner, working to the curve of the front flap. Pick up the first set of stitching threads and work across the front curve, ending when you meet the stitching on the opposite side. Secure the stitching threads and cut off any excess.

> **⌘ TIP ⌘** Because leather is so pliable a surface, if you work your stitching along one long side, then across the curvature of the front, and then down the second side, you can easily distort or twist the leather. Stitching side-to-front-to-side pulls your leather on the bias. Working one side and then the other evenly pulls both sides toward the front curve.

6 Slide one 1¼" (32mm) copper ring onto a strap loop. Place one end of the strap loop inside the purse and fold the other end over the outside of the purse, tanned leather side up. Slide the post of your screw-post rivet through the outer strap hole—the hole in the purse side—and then through the inner strap loop hole. Attach the screw cap to the screw-post rivet. Repeat for the second strap loop.

7 Attach the ends of each length of copper chain to the eye of the swivel latch, using one latch on each end of the chain and using a split ring as your joiner. Clip the swivel latches to the 1¼" (32mm) copper rings on one side of the purse.

8 With a lightly dampened sponge, moisten the inside—rawhide— of the flap where it will roll over the top of the purse. Gently roll the flap to the front of your purse. Lay the purse, flap down on your work table and allow it to dry overnight.

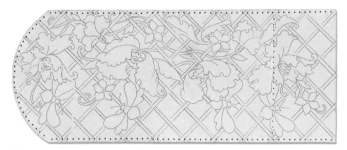

Figure 8.28. Preparation for the Pyrography Steps

Figure 8.29. Close-Up for Step 1

Figure 8.30. Outlining the Lattice Boards

Figure 8.31. Close-Up for Step 2

This project is burned more easily if you work the pyrography before the leathercrafting construction steps.

Pyrography Instructions

1 Cut, measure, and punch all holes in your leather pieces. Working on a grid-work cutting mat, align the diagonal lattice lines of the pattern to the leather along a 45-degree angle to the long side edge of the body piece. Using graphite paper, trace your pattern to the body of the lunch box purse. (See pattern, pp. 106–107.)

2 Set your temperature to a medium tonal-value heat. Lay a cork-backed metal ruler onto the pattern, aligning the ruler's edge next to, but not on, the lattice pattern lines. Allow the side of your medium writing tip or ball-tip pen to lightly touch the side of the ruler. Burn the lattice lines, using the ruler to keep your lines as straight as possible. You can work the lines in several layers of burning to achieve a dark, even tonal value.

> **TIP** A metal ruler can drain your pen tip of some of its heat. If your first burned line is very pale in tonal value, repeat the step without using the ruler. The indent in the leather surface that is created by the hot pen tip will keep your pen tip in line during the burning of the second layer.
>
> The cork backing of the metal ruler keeps the ruler from sliding or slipping from the pressure of the moving pen tip. If your metal ruler does not have a cork backing, use a small strip of 220-grit sandpaper folded lengthwise under your ruler. The sandpaper that faces up toward the ruler will hold the ruler in place on the paper, and the paper that faces down will hold the paper to the leather.
>
> Any pyrography pen gets hot enough to melt plastic rulers, so save them for your leather-cutting and pattern-tracing steps.

Figure 8.32. Working a Second Layer of Shading

Using a wide-ball tip or shading tip in your pyrography pen and a low–medium heat setting, work a layer of long, wide line shading into the flower petals, bumblebee wings and body, and leaves and stems. Follow the close-up *(see Fig. 8.33)* for placement. Work these shading strokes from the inner point of each element toward the outer edge of the element. For example, the bumblebee's wings are shaded from the point where the wings touch the body toward the outer rounded edges of the wings.

Repeat the shading process from step 3 to deepen the tonal values in each element. This second layer will create dark-toned beginnings to each shading stroke. Work one layer of shading on the lattice boards, using the same pen tip and heat setting. The lattice is shaded on the bottom where one lattice tucks under another.

Figure 8.33. Close-Up for Step 3

Figure 8.34. Adding a Third Layer of Shading to the Flower Petals

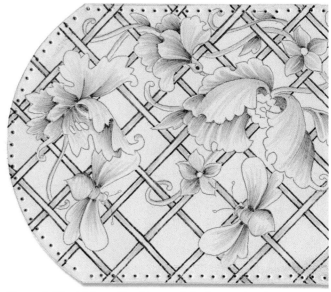

Figure 8.35. Adding a Third Layer of Shading to the Flower Petals

Figure 8.36. Outlining the Pattern Lines

Figure 8.37. Close-Up for Step 6

Figure 8.38. Solid-filling the Background

Figure 8.39. Close-Up for Step 7

5. A third layer of shading in the flower petals, leaves, and bumblebees creates darker tonal values at the beginning of the strokes. On each flower, one or two petals—the uppermost petals of the flower—are not worked with this step. That leaves those petals at a paler tonal value and therefore it appears as if those petals are closer to you than the darker-shaded petals.

6. Adjust the heat setting to a dark tonal value. Change your pyrography tip to a medium writing tip or ball-tip pen. Outline the pattern lines for all of the pattern elements. Add a few accent lines to the petals, working the lines with the direction of the curve of the petal. Add short line strokes to the bodies of the bumblebees to suggest stripes *(see Figs. 8.36 and 8.37)*.

7. The background space surrounding the design is solid-filled using a medium heat setting and the medium writing tip or ball-tip pen. Leave a thin line of unburned background around the bumblebee antennae. Work the background in multiple layers of tightly packed scrubbie strokes. The darkest tonal value for this step falls down the center line of the leather. As the background comes closer to the leather edges, the background has a paler tonal value *(see Figs. 8.38 and 8.39)*.

8. Using a document cleaning pad or white artist's eraser, remove any dirt and remaining tracing lines form your pyrography work. Remove the erasure dust using a dry, lint-free cloth.

> **TIP** In the close-up *(see Fig. 8.39)*, a thin, unburned halo is left around the bumblebee antennae. As the antennae and the background solid-fill are the same tonal value, the halo keeps the antennae from disappearing into the background work. If you have two areas of pyrography that touch and are the same tonal value, you can leave an unburned halo, or you can use the craft knife cutting technique that we used in the Practice Board Journal to cut the halo.

Figure 8.40. Adding Color with Colored Pencils

Using wax-based, artist-quality colored pencils, work two to three light coatings of each base-coat color into your design. For the large flowers the base coat is pale orange; the medium flowers is light purple; the small five-petal flowers is medium blue; the bumblebee wings is pale gray; the bumblebee bodies is golden yellow; and the leaves and stem is medium green. Gently dust the leather body to remove any colored pencil dust. Give the project one light coat of satin acrylic spray sealer or reworkable spray sealer to set this colored pencil work (*see Figs. 8.40 and 8.41*).

Work one to two more coatings of your base color for each area. Using complementary colors, add color changes in each area add one to two coats of colored pencil. For this burning, the large orange and medium-blue flowers and the bumblebee's body are accented with magenta; the leaves and stems, and small five-petal flowers are accented with turquoise; and the bee's wings and outer edges of the leaves are accented with white. Work two to three layers of purple into the flower centers (*see Figs. 8.42 and 8.43*).

Gently dust the leather to remove any colored pencil dust. Give the project one light coat of satin acrylic spray sealer or reworkable spray sealer to set this colored pencil work. When the spray coat is thoroughly dry, you can apply one or two coats of satin acrylic leather finish to protect your leather from dirt and water.

Return to Leathercrafting Instructions, steps 5–8, to complete the stitching of your lunch box purse.

Figure 8.41. Close-Up for Step 9

Figure 8.42. Final Colored Pencil Layers

Figure 8.43. Close-Up for Step 10

Mandala Lunch Box Purse — *Tonal Value Shading*

The Mandala Purse is also crafted in the lunch box style. Adult coloring books have captured the imagination of many people who have never worked on an arts and crafts project. One of the most popular themes of this style of art is the mandala—a circular geometric design that can include stylized natural elements. This trend inspired the Mandala Lunch Box Purse. Throughout the pyrography creation of this pattern, each area inside and outside the mandala pattern will be filled with solid-fill tonal values ranging from extremely pale to black tones.

Leathercrafting Instructions

NOTE: The pyrography steps for this project are easier to work before you do the leather construction steps for stitching and add the shoulder strap.

1 Cut the purse pieces from 6/7-ounce leather using a craft knife or rotary cutter, working on a self-healing cutting mat. Prepare the leather edges by trimming the sharp corners with the edge beveler and using Gum Tragacanth with the edge slicker to burnish the edges of each piece.

2 Because this project is worked in heavier-weight leather, cut the flap as a separate piece to the purse body. The join between the purse back and the purse flap helps the flap roll smoothly over the top of the purse. If you are working in lighter-weight leather, 5/6-ounce, you can join the pattern into one large piece by taping the paper pieces for the flap to the back, and aligning the flap bottom ½" (13mm) over the back.

3 The back edge of the flap overlaps the top edge of the back of the body—the flap lies on top of the body and the bottom edge of the flap sets ½" (13mm) down from the back top edge. Mark a stitching guide line on both pieces ¼" (6mm) from the overlapping edges. Mark the stitching holes at ¼" (6mm) intervals along these guidelines. Lay the two pieces, both tanned-side up, overlapping the flap on the back. Using a hand awl and a thick cork board, punch your stitching holes.

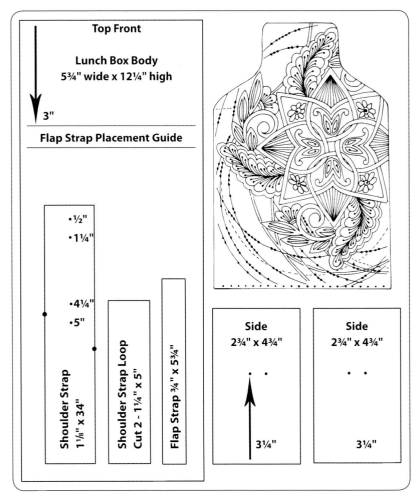

Figure 8.44. Mandala Lunch Box Purse, Leather Cutting Guide

4 Using waxed linen thread, two harness needles, and the double-needle stitch, join the purse flap to the top of the purse body.

5 Mark a pencil line along the outer edge of the back to create a stitching guide. The back will be stitched to the sides along both sides of the back piece. What appears to be the bottom edge of the purse body will roll around the purse sides to become the top inside edge of your purse. That top inside edge will not be stitched.

Mark your stitches at a ¼" interval. Using a hand awl and a thick cork board, punch the stitching holes. Also mark and punch the narrow edges of the flap strap for the stitching holes ¼" (6mm) from the edge at ¼" (6mm) intervals.

6 Work step 5 for the two side pieces. The stitching for these pieces is worked only on the two sides and the bottom. The top of the sides will not be stitched.

7 Following the cutting guide, and using the rotary punch set to fit your screw-post rivets, punch the rivet holes in the sides to secure the shoulder strap loops to the purse sides. Those holes are 3¼" (90mm) from the bottom edge and ¼" (6mm) off the center point.

8 Following the Leather Cutting Guide on page 79 and, using the rotary punch set to fit your screw-post rivets, punch the four holes in the shoulder strap loops. These holes are worked ½" (13mm) from each end and ¼" (6mm) off the center point.

9 Using a rotary punch set on the size that fits your single-cap rivets, mark and punch the four holes per side at the ends of the shoulder strap that will be used to secure the shoulder strap to the dee ring. Refer to the Cutting Guide for the measurements for the placement on the shoulder strap of these rivet holes.

> **⌘ TIP ⌘** Set your leathercrafting construction aside for the moment and move on to the pyrography steps for the purse flap. When you have completed the pyrography steps, begin your stitching steps. You will work through the stitching of the purse body to the sides as you did with the construction of the Flower Garden Purse. The stitching is broken down into small steps, and each step is worked on both sides before you move on to the next stitching step. By stitching both sides to the back, then both side bottoms to the purse bottom, and then both front sides to the purse side, you avoid distorting the leather into a bias-pulled twist.

10 Make a light pencil mark on the front of the purse body 3" (77mm) from the top edge on both sides of the body near the stitching holes. As you work the stitching steps to join the front to the sides, you will add the flap strap at this pencil-mark point and secure it as you stitch through all three layers of leather.

11 With waxed linen thread and two harness needles, use the double-needle stitch to join the purse body to the sides. To keep a square, lunch-box look to your purse, stitch one side edge of the purse to the back side of the body until you reach the bottom corner. Stop your stitching, but do not cut the threads.

12 Repeat this step for the opposite side, joining the body back along one side edge. Stop the stitching at the side corner, but do not cut the threads. You have one edge of both sides stitched to the body back at this stage, and you will have two sets of working thread hanging from both bottom corners.

13 Using a craft knife, make a small ¼" (6mm) cut at a 45-degree angle at the stitched bottom corner of the side. That small cut will allow you to ease the side corners as you turn the body of the purse around the square corner of the sides. Repeat for the second side. Do not cut the purse body.

14 Pick up your stitching threads and work the double-needle stitch across the bottom joint of the sides and purse body. Repeat this for the second side of the purse. Stop and drop the stitching thread at the second bottom corner.

Make a small ¼" (6mm), 45-degree-angle cut at the bottom corner of the sides to ease them as you roll the purse body forward.

 Pick up your dropped thread and, using the double-needle stitch, begin stitching the front of the purse body to the sides. Work the stitching until you reach the pencil mark for the flap strap.

 Hold the flap strap over the purse front and stitch through all three layers of leather. When the flap strap stitching is complete, continue the double-needle stitching to secure the remaining portion of the front to the side.

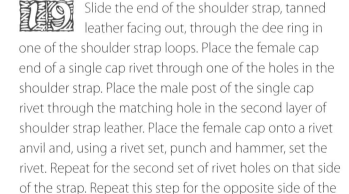 Fold the shoulder strap loops in half with the rawhide sides together and matching the punched holes. Slide one 1¼" (6mm) dee ring into the fold for each loop. Slide the posts of the screw-post rivets through both layers of the shoulder strap loop and then through the matching holes in the purse side. Place the screw cap of the screw-post rivets inside the purse and screw it tightly onto the screw post. Repeat this step for the second screw-post rivet. Repeat this step for the placement of the second shoulder strap loop on the second side of the purse.

 Slide the end of the shoulder strap, tanned leather facing out, through the dee ring in one of the shoulder strap loops. Place the female cap end of a single cap rivet through one of the holes in the shoulder strap. Place the male post of the single cap rivet through the matching hole in the second layer of shoulder strap leather. Place the female cap onto a rivet anvil and, using a rivet set, punch and hammer, set the rivet. Repeat for the second set of rivet holes on that side of the strap. Repeat this step for the opposite side of the shoulder strap.

Finish your Mandala Lunch Box Purse by applying two to three light coats of satin acrylic leather finish.

Stitching Guide

NOTE: Read steps 10 to 17 on pp. 80–81 before you begin the stitching process.

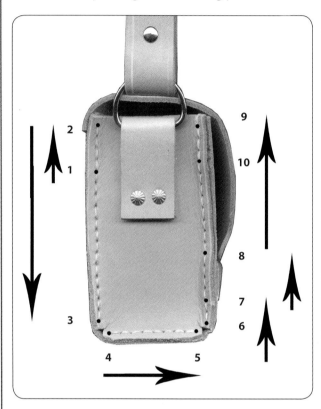

1. Begin the first stitch, centering the thread, 4 to 5 holes below the top edge of the back.
2. Stitch toward the top back edge.
3. Stitch from the top back edge to the bottom back corner; drop your threads. (Steps 11–12)
4. Clip the corner of the side piece ¼" (6mm); stitch across the bottom edge of the side; drop your threads.
5. Clip the corner of the side piece ¼" (6mm); stitch across the bottom edge of the side; drop your threads. (Steps 13–16)
6. Stitch to the front flap strap. (Step 17)
7. Stitch through all three layers of leather—side, front, and strap.
8. Stitch to top edge of the front.
9. Turn the direction of the stitching and backstitch 4 to 5 holes.
10. Secure the threads; trim the excess.

Figure 8.45. First Burning Layer of Tonal Value Work

Pyrography Instructions

Throughout this project, the background solid-fill textures are worked using a tightly packed circular or coils stroke. Because every area uses that texture, the tonal value of each area becomes visually more powerful than the actual method of burning the texture.

The background curved-line areas, shown in the background of the main mandala design, were established on the Mandala Purse by placing an 8" (203mm) round ceramic plate on the leather and then tracing along the outside edge of the plate with a soft #6–#8 pencil. Two of these background circles have extra wide ⅛" (3mm) borders.

NOTE: You can create your own background circles in this manner or refer to the original tracing pattern for those lines. Decide whether you will use the pattern background circles or create your own background circles before you begin the tracing step.

Trace the pattern *(see page 108)* to the leather using graphite paper. Work this first layer of burning on a low to low-medium temperature setting and use the medium writing tip, ball tip, or micro-writing-tip pen. Work one layer of tightly packed circles and coils to the spaces inside of the mandala teardrop shapes. Do not work the design patterns or the outline of the teardrops. Work one layer of circles and coils in the background space outside the mandala design. Darken the tonal value of the background space that is nearest the mandala design *(see Fig. 8.45 for exact position)* by laying down one to two more burnings of circles and coils.

Once you have the background circle lines marked, begin burning inside these circles, treating each one as a separate unit *(see Fig. 8.46)*. Work your circle-and-coil texturing inside of each circle, concentrating the texture near the circle outline. Work the two circle border lines with only one layer of circle-and-coil texture in the bottom half of the pattern. In the upper half of the pattern, these two border lines have two layers of burning. Note that throughout the burning these two borders remain in a pale tonal value.

> **TIP** When one circle overlaps another, treat the circle you are working on as if it were an independent pattern. This will give some areas of the background, where one circle overlaps another, multiple layers of the circle and coil texture stroke. You will texture that overlap once for the first circle, then again for the next circle. So where each circle may have two or three layers of texture work, the overlap area will have four to five layers, making the overlaps take on a deeper tonal value *(see Fig. 8.46)*.

Turn the heat setting of your pyrography tool up to a medium temperature. Work two to three layers of tightly packed circles and coils into the background areas of the main mandala pattern. Refer to Figure 8.47 for the placement of this darker work. Work a fourth layer of circle-and-coil texture in the background of the four small diamond shapes.

Using the medium writing tip or the ball tip at the medium temperature setting, pull several long, thin lines inside the petal shapes of the curved fern leaves. These lines begin at the base of the curved leaflet and are pulled to the halfway point inside that leaf. In the three curved leaflet shapes at the top of the spear-leaf stem shade the curved areas using long thin lines. Work these lines from the base of the curved leaflets into the midpoint of each leaf area.

Figure 8.46. Adding Dimension to the Background

Figure 8.47. Darkening the Inner Mandala Tonal Values

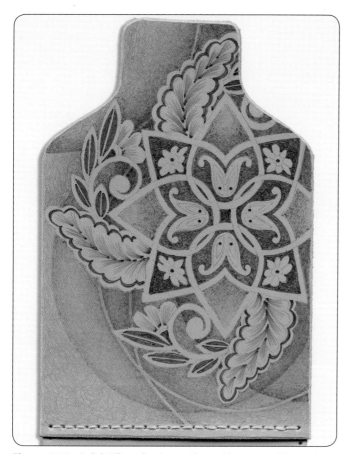

Figure 8.48. Solid-Filling the Spear-Shaped Leaves and Curved Fern Leaves Border

4 Using the tightly packed circle-and-coil texture, fill the spear-shaped leaf areas inside the spear leaf border with a solid-fill *(see Fig. 8.48)*. Use several layers to achieve a medium-dark tonal value. Fill the border lines of the curved fern leaves with this same tightly packed circle-and-coil stroke. Again, work several layers until you have a medium-dark tonal value.

5 With the medium writing tip or the ball tip on a medium-hot temperature setting, outline the tracing lines of the mandala pattern *(see Fig. 8.49)*. Do not outline the background circles.

Turn the heat down to a low-medium temperature setting. Using a light pressure on the medium writing tip or ball tip to create extra-thin lines, work one layer of short lines in the mandala borders to those borders that tuck under another border. Keep the shading closer to the overlap area and allow the borders that cross over another border line to remain unburned.

6 With the medium writing tip or ball-tip pen set on a medium-high heat setting, add the detail accents—long lines that follow the curves of the space—to the four larger diamond-shaped points along the outside of the mandala pattern. In each curved leaf of the curved fern, work two accent lines that start at the base of the curve and reach about two-thirds up into the curve. Each line is topped with a medium-sized dot. The outer section of the spear-shaped leaves has three medium dots inside the solid-fill area *(see Fig. 8.50)*.

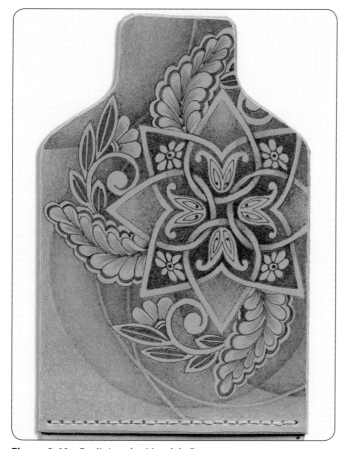

Figure 8.49. Outlining the Mandala Pattern

With the medium writing tip or ball-tip pen set on a medium-high temperature setting, rework the tonal values in the background space to bring these values into the very dark tones. To create a graduated tonal-value effect to the entire background area, these extra dark areas fall in the upper right-hand corner, with the blackest value falling in the leather curve for the flap tongue. Refer to Figure 8.50 to see the placement for this step.

To complete the mandala burning, lay an 8" (203mm) ceramic plate onto the purse flap. Orient the plate so that the outer edge lies over the left side of the leather, and the right edge of the plate is off the leather. Using your medium writing tip or the ball tip on a high temperature setting, place the tip lightly against the plate edge and pull your burning line using the plate's edge as a guide. Because the ceramic plate pulls heat from your burning tip, this line will be thin and pale and may have areas that do not burn at all. Adjust the plate slightly to offset it from the first circular line and pull a new line. Repeat, adding about 8 to 10 lines in the left background space.

With the medium writing tip or ball-tip pen on a high temperature setting, add touch-and-lift dots to all of the plate lines. Add these dots in small clusters of 3 to 5 spots in a tight spacing, then allow a space on the line without dots, and then create a new cluster *(see Fig. 8.51)*.

Clean the dry remaining tracing lines using a document cleaning pad, or a synthetic all-purpose eraser. Remove the eraser dust with a dry, lint-free cloth. When the burning is complete, return to the leather construction, steps 10–20 *(pages 80–81)*.

Figure 8.50. Detailing the Mandala Pattern

Figure 8.51. Adding the Rings

Winged Wood Spirit Journal — *Tonal-Value Shading*

While this project may appear far too complicated for a beginner, it uses a Simple Shading Formula that is easy to work, gives great results every time, and can be used with any pattern.

Supplies

See Basic Supply Lists, p. v

◇ Low-range, one-temperature pyrography tools

◇ Pyrography pen tips— wide-ball, medium writing tip, micro-ball tip

◇ Pyrography tip cleaning supplies

◇ 6/7-ounce vegetable-tanned leather

◇ 1—10½" (267mm) x 8½" (216mm) for journal cover

◇ 2—8½" (216mm) x 3" (77mm) for inside pockets

◇ Waxed linen thread

◇ 2 Harness or tapestry needles

Leathercrafting Instructions

Cut the pieces for your Winged Wood Spirit Journal; then work the pyrography steps before assembling the leather journal. Following the general leather construction steps for the Pyrography Practice Board in Chapter 7, cut and assemble your journal.

Retracing Small Pattern Areas

NOTE: When I first drew this design, the Wood Spirit did not have feathers above his eyebrows. After I had traced the project pattern and worked through the first two layers of shading to the face and feathers, I decided that the Wood Spirit needed those feathers to balance the visual weight of the extended wings. As you read through the steps you can see that steps 1 through 3 do not show the eyebrow feathers. At step 4 they will appear, and you will work through their shading steps.

To add those new feathers to my leather project, I traced the pattern *(see page 112)* onto semi-transparent vellum. Next, I traced the eyebrow feathers that I had added to the original drawing onto the vellum where they belonged in relation to the original pattern. Since the vellum is semi-transparent, it was easy to position this small pattern over the work I had already accomplished. Two pieces of low-tack painter's tape held the small pattern in place as I traced the new feathers to the leather using graphite paper.

Using graphite paper, trace the Winged Wood Spirit pattern to the front cover of your journal. Note that in the tracing pattern the detail lines and accent lines are not included. You will be working these lines free-hand. Your tracing pattern includes the eyebrow feathers discussed in Retracing Small Pattern Areas, above.

Figure 8.52. You can add new elements, readjust your tracing lines, and even retrace areas of a pattern onto your leather at any time in the pyrography process. Mid-and dark-toned shading can overpower your initial tracing lines, covering them enough that those lines are no longer visible. If this happens, simply cut that portion of the design from your pattern paper and, using graphite paper, retrace the lines over the burned tonal-value work.

Simple Shading Formula

The simple shading technique works all of the shading steps according to how one element in the pattern touches or tucks under another. In this pattern, the Winged Wood Spirit, all of the shading strokes begin at the element's edge closest to the center of the design. This leaves each element's farthest point from the design in an unburned or pale-toned value. For a pattern of ox-eyed daisies, each daisy petal will be worked from where the petal touches the flower center out to the end of the petal; the leaves will be worked from where they join the main leaf stem out to the outer edge of the leaf.

As layers of shading are worked within one element, the tonal-value coloring is graduated from darkest at the inner edge of the element to unburned at the outer tip of the element.

The simple shading technique consists of five simple steps:

1. The first shading is done with a wide-flat shader or wide-ball tip and is worked three-quarters of the way through the element.
2. The second shading is done with a medium ball tip and is worked halfway through the element.
3. The third shading also uses the medium ball tip and is worked one-quarter of the way through the element.
4. Solid-fill areas of black are worked using the touch-and-lift dot pattern and the medium ball tip.
5. The detailing and fine-line accents are worked using a micro-ball tip.

Using these five simple steps, you can turn any pattern into a leather pyrography masterpiece!

Figure 8.53. Wide-Line Shading

Figure 8.54. Simple shading is created without regard to a light source. Instead, the shading lines begin inside of an element where it touches or tucks under another element *(see Simple Shading Formula, page 87)* The stroke is pulled through the element to the mid-central point of the element, and it follows the curve of the element. If you look at the ball area of the nose in this close-up, you will see that the simple shading begins at the outside edge of the nostrils where they touch the side of the cheek, and then rolls in the same curved line shape as the pattern line that defines the top of the nostrils.

Using the medium ball tip in your low-range, one-temperature pyrography tool, begin this burning with a wide-line shading *(see Fig. 8.53)*. Use a gentle, light touch to the surface of the leather to burn pale tonal values into the face, wings, and corner accents elements. Create each shading stroke following the curve or direction of the larger area being shaded. All elements in the pattern receive some pale-tone shading during this step except for the eyes and nostrils.

> *∾ TIP ∾* This first layer of pale tonal-value shading establishes the depth of each element to the face or wing; it is a guide map for the more complex shading you will be working in the next few steps. Mapping an area or a full pattern first in pale-values tone allows you to see how clumps or groupings of elements interact within the pattern and help you see where you will want to work your mid-tone and dark-tone values.

The beginning of the wide-line shading strokes for all elements in the face starts at the closest point in the element at the center of the face. The beginning point for the shading in the individual feathers is where the feather is connected to the main wing. Finally, the shading in the leaves starts at the center vein of the leaf and is worked toward the outer edge of the leaf.

The hair is divided into small areas that will become individual clumps of hair within the larger hair section. In the close-up photo you can see that the mustache is created in two parts—one part of the mustache flows from the center of the face toward the left side, and the other section flows from the center of the face toward the right side. Each mustache section is further broken down into smaller elements. For example, the mustache grouping that comes from the base of the nose is made up of four separate hair elements.

As you work this and all other shading steps, allow one edge of each hair element to remain unburned. The rounded scroll ends of all of the hair elements are never shaded and remain at the white tonal value of the leather coloring. This includes the hair found in the mustache, beard, sideburns, and in the eyebrows. These white unburned lines within each hair element are easiest to location in the finished project's close-up in step 10.

This step focuses on the face (see Figs. 8.55 and 8.56). Unplug your pyrography tool and allow it to cool. Remove the wide-ball tip and replace it with the medium ball tip. Re-plug your tool and allow it to reach full temperature. Throughout this step, use a slow movement with your pen tip to allow the thin-line shading to reach mid- and dark-tone values.

Work a second layer of shading to the pale tonal value shading from step 1. Use thin-line shading that follows the general curve of each area. Work these lines slightly shorter than the first layer of work; this allows a portion of pale value to remain above the darker tonal lines.

The eyebrows are worked with the thin-line shading starting at the bottom of the brow and reaching toward the forehead. The upper eye has this new layer of shading worked from the corner of eyelid by the nose out toward the brow line. The side eye wrinkles are shaded from the outer edge of the eye toward the hair line. The lower eyelid is shaded first on the inner corner where it touches the upper eyelid, and then again at the outer corner where it touches the side wrinkles. Both sets of shading for the lower eyelid are pulled toward the center.

The second layer of fine-line shading for the mustache, beard, and hair is worked directly over the first layer of wide-line shading. Keep this layer slightly shorter than the first to allow some of the original pale tonal value to remain. The side of the face has two cheek sections, one near the eye and one near the nose. Both cheek sections are worked over the first layer of wide-line shading along the hairline area. There is no shading on these two areas on the inner portion of the cheeks.

Using a touch-and-lift dot pattern, fill the black iris area of the eye, leaving the eye highlight unburned. Add fine, thin lines to the pupil radiating out to the outer edge of the iris. Pull one even-toned line along the top edge of the lower eyelid where it touches the eyeball. Fill the nostrils with a touch-and-lift dot to a solid-fill. Next to the nose nostrils in the lower cheek area are two small triangles, one on each side of the nose. Fill these triangles with solid touch-and-lift dots.

In Figure 8.56, you can see that about one-third to one-half of the elements in the face, mustache, and beard have no shading at this point and remain at the original tonal values of the leather surface.

Figure 8.55. Winged Wood Spirit Journal, Working the Face

Figure 8.56. Winged Wood Spirit Journal, Working the Face, Close-Up

Figure 8.57. Winged Wood Spirit Journal, Fine-Line Shading

Figure 8.58. Winged Wood Spirit Journal, Fine-Line Shading

Figure 8.59. Winged Wood Spirit Journal, Close-Up

A third layer of fine-line shading is added to the face during this step. This layer will establish the darkest tonal values of the face—not every area of the face is worked.

Add a new layer of fine-line shading to the lower fourth of the eyebrows. Add a new layer of shading to the inside corners of the upper and lower eyelids. Work one more layer along the outside edges of the nose.

Looking at Figures 8.57 and 8.58, you can see that on each side of the Wood Spirit's face the hair is clumped into three distinct groups—the mustache, the beard hair, and the sideburn hair. Treat all of the elements that make up the sideburn hair grouping as one element. Work a new layer of shading over all of the small elements inside this grouping. This new layer begins at the face and reaches about one-quarter of the way out. Repeat this for the sideburn hair on the opposite side of the face. Repeat this new layer burning for the two beard-hair groupings.

Work one layer of new fine-line shading into each of the elements of the mustache, with the darkest values of the layer at the central part of the mustache.

> ⟞ **TIP** ⟝ By grouping small elements into one large element and then working a layer of shading over the entire group, you soften, blend, and darken the edges of each element slightly and unite them visually. When you compare the mustache, worked as an individual element, to the beard and sideburns, the mustache is pushed forward visually in the burning because it still has the clean white-toned lines on each of the elements that make up that area.

Refer to Retracing Small Pattern Areas on page 87. Replace your medium ball tip with the wide-ball tip. Work a layer of wide-ball tip shading into the eyebrow feathers. The shading is worked from the closest point of the feathers to the face and reaches about three-quarters of the way up toward the outer point of the feathers.

Replace your wide-ball tip with the medium ball tip and, using fine-line shading, burn a second layering of mid-tone shading to these same eyebrow feathers. End this shading about one-half of the way into each feather toward the feather's point. Work a third layer of shading, using the medium ball tip and working this layer only one-quarter of the way through each feather.

Replace your wide-ball tip for the medium ball tip and work a layer of fine-line shading. This layer of shading is worked in each element and covers the bottom fourth of the feather area where it is closest to the face.

Using the medium ball tip, work a new layer of shading over the wide-ball tip shading into the feathers, starting at the edge of each feather that is closest to the face and working toward the outer point of the feather. This layer fills about one-half of each feather.

Add a third layer of shading, using the medium ball tip and working this layer in the same manner as the rest of the shading; bring the shading about one-quarter of the way toward the feather points *(see Fig. 8.61)*.

Figure 8.60. Winged Wood Spirit Journal, Mid-Tone and Fine-Line Shading

Figure 8.61. Winged Wood Spirit Journal, Close-Up

Figure 8.62. Winged Wood Spirit Journal, Feathers

Figure 8.63. Winged Wood Spirit Journal, Feathers Close-Up

⑨ Replace the medium ball tip with the micro-ball tip. Using a pencil, draw a line down the center of the largest feathers in the wings, using Figure 8.62 for placement. The large feather details are burned in two steps: Work along one side of the pencil line; fill that side with the detail lines. Then work the second side of the feather, again working from the pencil line. Begin adding detailing to these feathers by burning thin, fine lines that start at the pencil line and are pulled to the feather's edge at a slight outward angle. Allow a line's width of space between each burned line. The two sets of detail lines in the large feathers will create a "herringbone pattern" that runs down the center of the feather.

Repeat this process with the smaller feathers that lie under the large feathers. Begin by making a pencil line down the center of the feather, and then work two rows of fine detail lines from that center line to the outer edge of the feathers.

There are a few small feathers in the wing structure that are either too small for two sets of detail lines or are located where only one side of the feather shows. For these feathers, work one set of detail lines from where the feather tucks under the adjacent feather out toward the point of the feather.

Where necessary, outline the edges of the feathers. Refer to Figure 8.63 for this step to see how very few outlines are needed to create a strong "feather look" or to separate one feather from another.

10 The eyebrow feathers are worked exactly as you worked the wing feathers in step 9. With the micro-ball tip, add strong accent lines to the eyelids, the sides of the nose, and the ball tip of the nose, where it joins the mustache. Several wrinkle lines are accented in the bridge area of the nose. Work a thin detailing line along the outer edge of the eye's pupil. The bottom cheek area, directly under the lower eyelid, is accented, but this accent line does not extend beyond the edge of the eyelid.

In this step we will treat the hair as individual elements instead of groupings. Work each element as one unit; then move into the next hair element area. Fill each hair element with long, thin lines that are burned from the edge or point nearest the face toward the outer point of the element. Accent the ends of each hair cluster with a fine detailing line so that the unburned lines and round scroll ends are outlined.

In the corner and line pattern on the back section of the journal cover, add fine-line detailing to each leaf using the same center pencil line and two sets of lines that are worked from the pencil line toward the leaf edge. Pull an accent line over the center pencil line to create a center vein. Work the scroll lines with thin accent lines along the outer edges. Allow a few areas of these scroll lines—areas where the shading steps are strong—to have no accent line. Touch-and-quick-pull stroke comma accents are worked using the micro-ball tip in the background area of the scroll lines for a touch of added interest. Refer to Figure 8.65 for the placement of these quick comma strokes.

11 Using a synthetic all-purpose eraser or a white artist's eraser, remove any dirt and tracing lines from your pyrography. Remove the eraser dust using a dry, lint-free cloth.

12 Return to the steps in the Practice Board Journal on pages 47 to 49 to complete the leather construction for this project. Finish the stitched leather journal using two to three light coats of satin acrylic leather finish.

Figure 8.64. Winged Wood Spirit Journal, Facial Details, Hair, and Leaves

Figure 8.65. Winged Wood Spirit Journal, Close-Up

Read with Me Owl Wristband/Bookmark — *Adding Detailing, Solid-Fill*

Small spaces can take very detailed burnings. This little owl completely fills the space of the wristband/bookmark. Every area of the leather has been burned with detailing, solid-fill, or textured shading.

Supplies

See Basic Supply Lists, p. v

◇ 1—2¼" (57mm) x 9" (229mm) long, 5/6 ounce leather

◇ Variable-temperature pyrography unit

◇ Medium writing tip or ball tip

1 Cut the wristband/bookmark from lightweight 5/6-ounce vegetable-tanned leather. If you are working this project as a wristband, punch two ⅛" (3mm) holes on each end of the band to accept ⅛" (3mm) suede lacing. Trace the pattern (p. 99) to the leather using graphite paper, tracing only the basic outlines.

2 Set your variable-temperature pyrography tool to a medium heat level. Using the medium writing pen or ball-tip pen and a tightly packed scrubbie stroke, work the shading into the upper and lower eyelid areas. Work this first layer starting at the outer corners and moving toward the center point of each eyelid. Work a second layer of shading at the outer corners of each area to darken those areas.

3 Using the same temperature setting, work the scrubbie stroke in the lower background area of the breast feathers. This tonal value is as dark as the inner eyelid corners. Use tightly packed fine lines, worked from the top of each feather toward the bottom edge of the feather, to shade the individual breast feathers.

4 Shade the outer edge of the eye's iris with the tightly packed scrubbie stroke. The darkest area of this shading is toward the outer edges of the iris, just under the upper eyelids. Repeat this shading in the white area of the eyes. Outline the pupil, iris, and square highlight in the pupils with a dark-toned line. You can re-burn these lines several times to bring the line into the black tones. Fill the pupil area with tightly packed touch-and-lift dots until the area reaches a black tonal value. Burn fine lines into the iris radiating around the eye's pupil. Outline the beak, beak feathers, eye feathers, and wing feathers.

5 Using the same temperature setting and the medium-writing or ball-tip pen, fill the feathers with some fun line patterns. For my small feathers I chose diagonally worked, short, parallel lines. The wing feathers were worked in 90-degree angled lines and then a small black spot was burned at the 90-degree-angle point. Burn the ring of medium-sized dots above and below the eye to a black tonal value.

Figure 8.66. This project, which began as a wristband, became a bookmark. The small holes on each end of the leather were punched to receive ⅛" (3mm) suede leather lacing for the wristband ties.

Figure 8.67. The dark solid-fill pupils of the eye are the focal point of this pattern.

Figure 8.68. To make the small breast feathers puff out from the chest, a dark tonal value is worked in the lower background area of the breast. The dark background tones make the breast feathers appear lighter in tonal value then they really are.

Figure 8.69. This owl's pupils are the darkest tonal value in the entire work. Inside the pupils is one small square of unburned leather that becomes the eye's highlight.

Figure 8.70. Since the owl has a fun look, whimsical line patterns can be used to detail the feathers.

NOTE: The background area surrounding this owl pattern was burned to a deep mid-tone value using the tightly packed scrubbie stroke. Remove any dirt and remaining tracing lines using a document cleaning pad or a white artist's eraser. Remove any eraser dust with a dry, lint-free cloth. Brush on one to three coats of satin acrylic leather finish.

Project Patterns

The project patterns include both basic outlines and fine detailing.
You can trace the outlines only for your first pyrography steps; the fine
detail lines can be added later by cutting small portions of the pattern
and spot-tracing the lines, or by free-handing them.

Many of the patterns, such as the Read with Me Owl Wristband/
Bookmark, can be used over and over. This project was worked as an
outlined design with a solid-fill background, but you can burn it using
fill textures. And the same fine-line shading used in the Carousel Horse
Book Cover can be used to create the Desert Landscape.

Narrow Bracelets

Leather Wristbands
(p. 17)

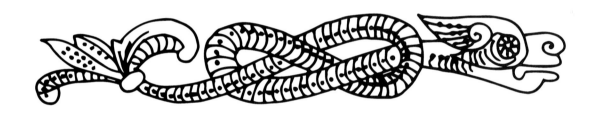

Double-Needle Stitching Patterns
(p. 40)

Henna Tattoo Wristband
(p. 15)

**Read with Me Owl
Wristband/Bookmark**
(pp. 94–95)

**Practice Grid
Wristband**
(p. 45)

**Leaf and Berries
Wristband**
(p. 43)

Project Patterns **99**

**Mayan
Wristband**
(p. 10)

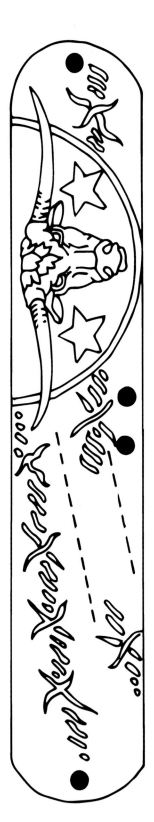

**Texas Longhorn
Wristband**
(p. 26)

A A A B β B C C C
D D D E E E F F F
G G G H H H I I J J
K K K L L L M M 3
N N N O O O P P
Q Q Q R R R S S S
I I T T T U U V V
W W X X X Y Y Z
1 2 3 4 5 6 7 8 9 0 0

✳ ◇ → ☆ ☽ ⌒

**Mayan
Boot Belt**
(p. 43)

**North American
Indian Boot Belt**
(p. 43)

Oriental Dragon
Boot Belt
(p. 43)

Desert Landscape
Journal
(pp. 64–70)

Parrot Key Tag
(p. 10)

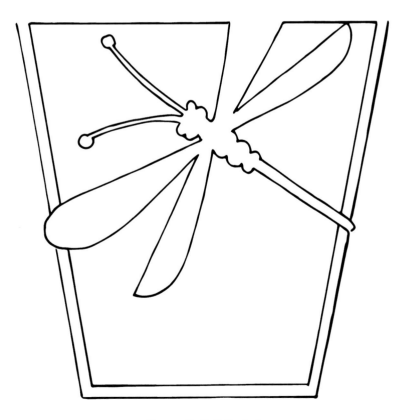

Dragonfly Belt Pocket
(p. 16)

Neo-Tribal Tattoo Wristband
(p. 15)

Butterfly Hat Band
(p. 19)

Butterfly Hat Band
(p. 19)

Flower Garden Lunch Box Purse
(pp. 71–77)

Flower Garden Lunch Box Purse
(pp. 71–77)

Mandala Lunch Box Purse

(pp. 78–85)

Wild Rose and Practice Board Journal
(pp. 46–55)

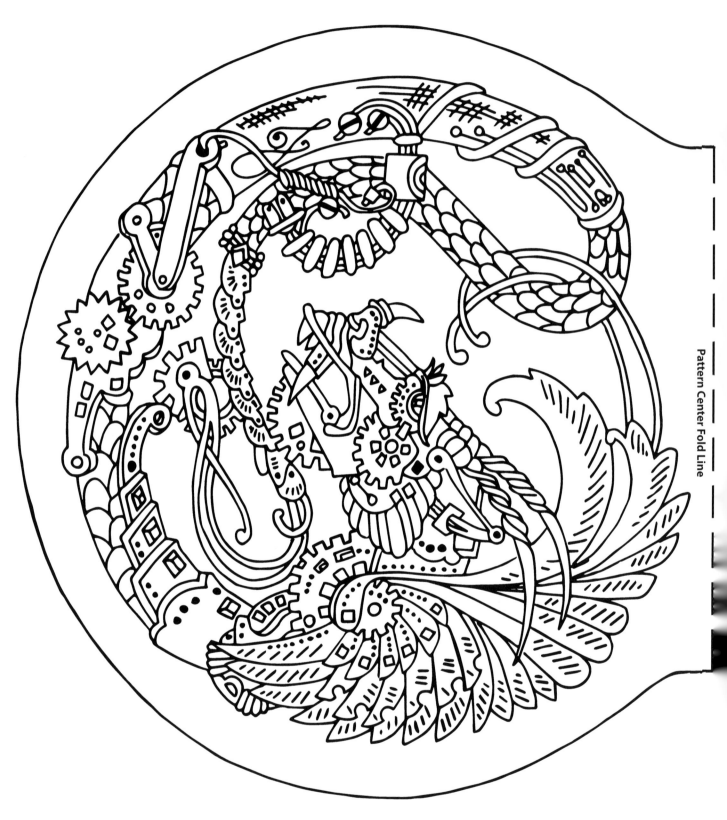

Pattern Center Fold Line

Steampunk Dragon Purse

(pp. 61–63)

Steampunk Dragon Purse
(pp. 61–63)

Winged Wood Spirit Journal
(pp. 86–93)

The Art of Leather Burning

Pink Petals Key Tag
(pp. 11–13)

Dragon Round
(p. 22)

Made in the USA Key Tag
(p. 19)

**Pink Henna
Flower Key Tag**
(p. 10)

**Yellow Henna
Flower Key Tag**
(p. 10)

Numbered Key Tags

(p. 23)

Daisy Key Tag

(p. 21)

Hair Barrettes, Necklaces

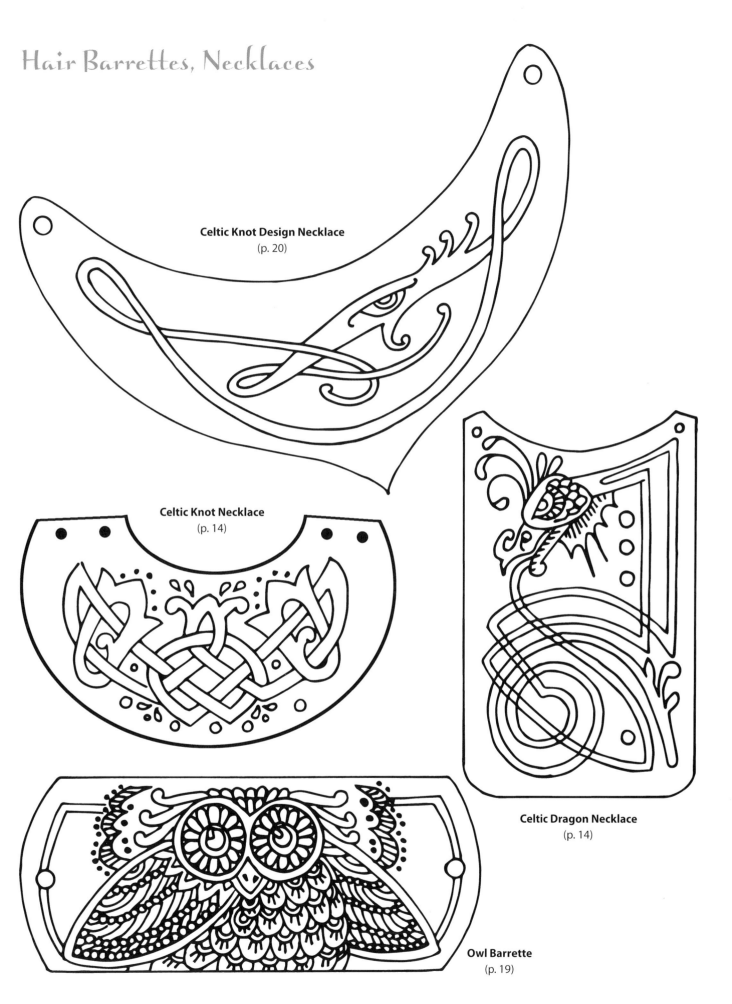

Celtic Knot Design Necklace
(p. 20)

Celtic Knot Necklace
(p. 14)

Celtic Dragon Necklace
(p. 14)

Owl Barrette
(p. 19)

Desert Landscape Journal
(pp. 64–70)

Desert Landscape Journal
(pp. 64–70)

Steampunk Belt Pocket
(p. 25)

Feathered Wristband
(p. 43)

Scrap Bag Hair Clip
(p. 45)

Carousel Horse Book Cover
(pp. 57–60)